Rojava

An Alternative to Imperialism, Nationalism, and Islamism in the Middle East

(*An introduction*)

By Oso Sabio

To all of the independent reporters, activists, and academics who
keep facts flowing unrestricted throughout the world;

To all of those who believe that a freer and fairer world is possible;

To all of those who have given their lives for that dream in the past;

To all of those who fight to make that vision a reality today;

To my family, without which I would not be the person I am today;

And to Cristina, for her love and support while I wrote this book;

Thank you!

ISBN 978-1-326-45480-7

9 781326 454807

Index

Introduction

In a beautifully diverse territory not too far away from our own, human communities have shaped the environment around them. Within these settlements, **the strong, the deceptive**, or **the exploitative** usually have political power. Those with different physical features, cultural traditions, or religious beliefs from these elites, meanwhile, find themselves treated, more often than not, as second-class citizens in their own community. At the same time, women (and children) are usually confined to unpaid labour, considered to be objects in the service of men, deprived of a say in how their lives will unfold, or given less recognition for their work than they deserve. In many cases, they are essentially society's third-class citizens.

In one settlement, the elite claims that it knows best, that its system of government is the most advanced, and that its interference in the affairs of other communities is essentially a form of charity. It argues that its support for repressive rulers in other settlements is justified, that its plots to disempower their people are in their best interests, and that its own population would be under threat if it didn't interfere as much as did.

In a neighbouring community, the elite asserts that it speaks on behalf of a deity, and that only its system of government can ensure protection, justice, and eternal salvation for its citizens. Those in the settlement who believe in a different deity, or in no deity at all, either have to submit to the elite's rule, leave their homes, or face execution.

Elsewhere, the elite says that its ethnic group is superior to others, and that it will protect all of those within that group (from outside forces or 'internal enemies') as long as they don't question its leadership. Those in the settlement who belong to a different ethnic group or have different physical features may be respected to a certain extent if they submit to the elite's rule, but they may also be called traitors whenever they question the elite or whenever the elite starts to lose the faith of its ethnic supporters. In the latter case, they are usually oppressed, humiliated, exploited, or even killed.

In another settlement, the elite maintains that every citizen is equal, that those seeking to interfere in their affairs have to be stopped, and that it is the force most able to stop foreign aggressors. It claims that only it knows how best to guide the community towards justice and peace, and that those who challenge it are traitors to their people. In reality, however, it exploits and deceives its own citizens by constantly generating fear and by controlling both their minds and actions.

In the final community, there is no elite. Unity and self-protection stop the strong from ruling through fear and external aggressors from asserting control. Education and independent thought, meanwhile, prevent demagogues from ruling through deception, while popular control of common resources (together with cooperative organisation) ensures that the exploitative cannot join forces with the strong and deceptive to establish dominance.

At the same time, each citizen considers their neighbours as their equals, whether they live in their own community or in neighbouring communities. Differences in physical features, cultural traditions, or religious beliefs have no impact on this egalitarian treatment. Children, women, and men, meanwhile, are all seen to deserve the same amount of respect. In short, everyone has control over their own destinies, and no-one is oppressed.

The above examples are all interpretations of currently- or historically-existing political systems, including: imperialism; theocracy; ethnic and civic nationalism; liberalism; authoritarian 'communism'; and libertarian socialism. The 'communities' and 'settlements', however, would be called countries or nations in today's world.

Through the process of investigation I undertook before publishing *Rojava: An Alternative to Imperialism, Nationalism, and Islamism in the Middle East,*[1] I realised how similar many statist ideologies are. The very nature of centralising power seemed inevitably to take democratic control away from citizens – no matter the project the different societal elites had in mind. The Rojava Revolution, on the other hand, appeared to break away from a number of historical traditions.

Having learned of an inspirational experience in the middle of a chaotic post-Arab Spring environment, I now began to analyse its value by looking more closely at the context. Firstly, I gave an overview of the key events in the Middle East between the twentieth and twenty-first centuries, including the rise and fall of Arab nationalism in Egypt and the phenomenon of Ba'athism in Syria and Iraq. Then, I explored the nature of the 'Kurdish Question', and how the fight for autonomy developed after Kurdish communities had been absorbed into the new regional states set up by different ethnic groups (often with European support).

Subsequently, I explained how the power of Saudi Arabia and its school of Islam began to grow with British and US help, and how Iran and its school of Islam rose as a reaction to imperialist interference in the region. I then analysed how US wars in the Middle East (in addition to those launched by Israel) had destabilised the region, fuelling discontent and

[1] http://www.lulu.com/shop/http://www.lulu.com/shop/oso-sabio/rojava-an-alternative-to-imperialism-nationalism-and-islamism-in-the-middle-east/paperback/product-22396254.html?ppn=1

helping to radicalise sectors of its population. I also examined the increasingly spontaneous actions of civilians in the Arab Spring, and how the lack of significant organisation allowed Western-backed Islamist forces to appropriate the uprisings for themselves.

I then examined in further depth the phenomenon of Daesh (or ISIS), which presented itself as a brutal and quasi-fascist reaction to imperialist interference in the Muslim World. In particular, I focussed on how the West and its Middle Eastern allies played a key role in facilitating the growth of the jihadist group. This analysis then led to an evaluation of the Left's stance on the Syrian Civil War, and why the rhetoric of imperialists against anti-imperialists was both simplistic and counterproductive.

Finally, I looked at the development of the Kurdish PKK rebels in Turkey, and the subsequent growth of a truly alternative force for change in the Middle East which worried imperialists, nationalists, and Islamists alike (though to differing extents). In particular, I explored the Rojava Revolution of northern Syria in greater detail, evaluating how it had developed and how other forces had responded to it.

With the PKK and its Rojavan allies heroically resisting both Daesh and the hostility of other forces surrounding them in Syria and Iraq, the international context got a lot more complicated, with the USA, Turkey, and Iraqi Kurdistan responding in particular to the successful Rojavan resistance in the city of Kobanî. Could the Rojava Revolution and progressive forces elsewhere in the region survive? Could their belief in inclusivity and autonomy truly bring peace to the region? Those are the questions I sought to answer in my book. And, in this heavily summarised version of my investigation, I seek to make the facts much more accessible to readers who don't have time to read the original text.

1) How Nationalism Stepped into the Vacuum Left by the Collapse of the Ottoman Empire

The more we're divided,
The more we're exposed,
The more we lose freedom,
And the less we control.

The collapse of the Ottoman Empire at the start of the twentieth century left a **power vacuum** in the Middle East, and European colonial powers (or European-born political ideologies) quickly sought to fill this space. While Britain and France stepped in to control a significant amount of territory, though, some new countries also emerged. Most were governed by **repressive Western-backed dictators or monarchs** (primarily in the Gulf region), of which Saudi Arabia's would be a good example, but other regimes were driven more by nationalist sentiment. **Turkey and Iran**, for example, saw powerful military leaders (Mustafa Kemal **Atatürk** and Reza Khan) follow the nation-building ideology of Europe and repress minority groups in the process. During the **Second World War**, the regime of the former remained neutral right until 1945, while that of the latter actually allied itself with the Nazis.

Egypt, meanwhile, would also be at the forefront of constructing a new Middle East after the end of Ottoman dominance, perhaps because it had benefitted from a head start over its neighbours. The biggest change in the region, however, would come with **the formation of the State of Israel in 1948**. With colonial powers starting to leave the region and some Arab intellectuals still hoping for the creation of a unified Arab State, the insertion of a largely foreign force into the middle of Arab-populated territory seemed to suggest that colonialism was far from finished. As a result of the unpopular creation of the Zionist State, and the refugee crisis and colonial repression that had preceded it, **Arab nationalism** gained in strength, and a coalition of Arab countries launched an abortive offensive against the young Israeli nation.

The defeat of the Arab coalition by Israel sent shockwaves through the region, and nationalist fervour grew even more. In 1952, Gamal Abdel **Nasser** and other dissenting military officials in Egypt took power in a coup, aiming to decrease the influence of foreign powers on Egyptian soil. In Iran, meanwhile, Mohammad **Mosaddegh** would nationalise Iranian oil in 1951 and be overthrown two years later in a coup backed by the CIA and MI6.

When **Nasser nationalised the Suez Canal in 1956**, Israel invaded (being joined later by France and Britain) with the intention of overthrowing Nasser. However, the USSR, the USA, and the UN called on the colonial powers to withdraw their troops, and the repercussions would be immense. **Nasser became an inspiration** for people throughout the region, and anti-Zionist, anti-imperialist forces would rise to prominence in Syria, Iraq, Algeria, Tunisia, Yemen, and Libya (to name just the most influential).

Iraq, for example, saw Abd al-Karim **Qasim** (who, like Nasser, had served in the 1948 war against Israel) overthrow the country's monarchy. He nationalised Iraqi oil and implemented a number of progressive measures but, in **1963**, the **CIA supported a young Saddam Hussein** and his Iraqi Ba'ath Party in their murderous coup against the nationalist prime minister. This would soon be referred to as the agency's 'favourite coup'. In the same year, meanwhile, a more progressive wing of the Ba'ath Party would take power in Syria.

In **1967, Israel would wage another war** against its Arab neighbours, leaving them desolated and in increasing economic difficulties. One reaction to this event would be another Ba'athist coup in Iraq a year later, though the party would now implement progressive policies which worried the West and attracted support from the Soviet Union. In **1970**, however, Nasser died, and a more **right-wing and authoritarian** wing of the regime would soon take power. The same would happen in Syria, where **Hafez al-Assad** would lead a coup against the more progressive elements within the Syrian Ba'ath Party. Libya's Muammar **Gaddafi** would perhaps be the person to most continue with Nasser's legacy (undertaking nationalisations and supporting resistance movements throughout the world after his bloodless coup in **1969**).

Overall, the anti-imperialism of Nasser (and those like him) would inevitably end in increasing authoritarianism and repression because, along with constant interference from the USA, Israel, and former colonial nations, they had no real commitment to creating a truly independent working class. Essentially, they failed (or refused) to make a distinction between the exploiters and the exploited in society. And, as a result, they saw themselves controlling workers' organisations in the 'interest of national stability'. That is not to say, however, that there were no progressive intentions in certain sections of these political elites. There almost certainly were. Nonetheless, the lack of popular democracy, which was due in large part to a lack of independent thought and organisation, meant that their failure in the face of imperialist hostility was essentially inescapable.

Ba'athism thrived off the errors of Nasser's attempts at an 'inclusive' nationalism. In both Syria and Iraq, the Ba'athist state would eventually be run by small and repressive military cliques under the personality cult of a charismatic dictator –

though there were, in all fairness, some relatively progressive moments (in Syria in the 60s and in Iraq in the 70s). The parties of each country were also incredibly self-interested, and they competed with each other from the 60s onwards for ideological domination of the Palestinian resistance movement (a position originally held by Nasser). In spite of their reactionary characteristics and ethnic chauvinism, however, both Ba'ath parties would be supported by the Soviet Union as they were more progressive than other forces in the region.

At the same time, Kurds and other ethnic groups were absorbed into the territory of the new nation states in the Middle East after the fall of the Ottoman Empire. Suffering from an arbitrary division of land orchestrated by both European colonialists and local nationalists, Kurdish communities found themselves split primarily between Turkey, Iran, Syria, and Iraq. In the Turkish State, Atatürk had promised Kurdish leaders that if they supported his nation-building cause they would be rewarded with respect and a certain amount of autonomy, but he soon reneged on his assurance and tried to assimilate non-Turks to create a form of ethnic 'purity'. Similar processes would happen in the other countries in which Kurds resided, and resistance would inevitably follow. However, the call for a Kurdish nation would result in intense state repression of Kurdish communities (including a number of massacres).

With the Soviet Union often opting to support the nationalists in charge in the Middle East, Kurdish nationalists regularly found themselves courting the support of the USA, and even Israel. The Iraqi **KDP** (led first by Mustafa Barzani and then Masoud **Barzani**) would soon become the most powerful nationalist organisation after its foundation in 1946. At first, it received support from the USSR, but when Qasim received the superpower's blessing in the late 50s, the KDP increasingly began to seek Western backing. In the decades that followed, it would continue to put its desire of forming a state above any other political principle or ideology, speaking of ethnic unity and independence rather than justice for Kurdish workers.

The conservative tribal leadership of KDP, however, saw discontent grow in the mid-70s, and many Kurds began to look elsewhere for political change. While some Kurds had already played significant roles in communist organisations, others within the KDP itself were now becoming increasingly critical of the party's right-wing politics. In Iraq, the 'social democratic' PUK would soon form, while in Turkey the Marxist PKK (or Kurdistan Workers' Party) would rapidly gain prominence for its armed resistance against the repressive Turkish State.

The KDP and PUK would cooperate with the USA's invasion of Iraq in 2003, and would play a significant part in the following political order. Although they would maintain a democratic façade, they would also oversee the creation of a corrupt, Western-backed capitalist regime in the autonomous KRG of Iraq. At the same time, the PKK would move away from the nationalist and top-down ideology it had previously held, and would gain greater popularity as a result.

Overall, Middle Eastern nationalists had shown that, in spite of the implementation of a number of progressive measures, they never really had an interest in empowering their citizens by ensuring their democratic voice was heard. Nor did they really seek to give people control over the natural wealth in their respective countries or to end their exploitation at the hands of national capitalists. These elites claimed that they knew best how to bring about progress, and sought in this way to justify not listening or giving power to their citizens.

The truth was, however, that they did not know how to bring progress to the lives of their subjects. And, thanks to both ideological dogmatism and imperialist attempts to undermine them, they failed to bring justice and genuine equality to their countries. Consequently, many ordinary people were soon ready for a change. The existing secular organisations, though, had not proved very successful, and were thus no longer regarded as the vehicle for societal transformation.[2]

Without libertarian secularists offering a break from the authoritarian status quo, another ideology filled the vacuum of popular confidence. Just like nationalism had stepped in to offer a way forward after the collapse of the Ottoman Empire, a form of doctrinaire religious reaction would now seek to replace the old order. Political Islam, which had previously been supported by the West as a means of undermining independent or anti-imperialist movements in the Middle East, would now inspire citizens into action with its own promises of change.

---

[2] An in depth discussion of the links between imperialism and nationalism can be seen between Chapters 1 and 4 of *Rojava: An Alternative to Imperialism, Nationalism, and Islamism in the Middle East*

2) How Islamism Filled the Gap Left by Nationalism

When we go and plant a seed,
We're aware of what we've sown,
And when we play about with nature,
Nothing positive is grown.

The historical dynamic between the Christian and Muslim Worlds had long been one of colonial condescension from the former. Women's rights, for example, were spoken of as a great achievement of the West, even at a time when Western women were becoming more and more subjugated by encroaching industrialism. Nonetheless, religious fervour was encouraged by colonialists after the First World War as a political ideology preferable to that of secular progressivism. After the **violently puritanical and exclusionist Wahhabists** had taken Mecca and Medina thanks to an alliance with the tribe of Abdulaziz Ibn Saud in the mid-1920s, for instance, Great Britain soon stepped in to support the young nation of Saudi Arabia. The Wahhabi impulse (obliging followers to wage holy war) was now institutionalised by the House of Saud in an attempt to gain Western acceptance, and this form of religious extremism would soon be directed abroad.

With oil becoming a resource of great importance during the Second World War, meanwhile, the USA would also become a keen ally of the Saudi monarchy in an attempt to ensure that the Middle East's 'black gold' did not fall into the hands of pro-Soviet nationalists. According to Pulitzer Prize-winning journalist Steve Coll, **the UK and USA "supported right wing or religious... groups covertly or sometimes overtly"** on numerous occasions during the twentieth century in order to "stop modernist governments such as Nasser in Egypt or Gandhi in India as well as leftist oriented governments" in general. **Britain**, for example, "**certainly supported the**

Muslim Brotherhood as an instrument of challenge against Nasser", while "the Israelis supported Hamas covertly" during the 1980s in order to "create a rival movement within the Palestinian community against the [progressive] PLO".

When the communist **Saur Revolution** occurred in Afghanistan in 1978, this Western tactic intensified, with "Afghan factions allied to the US" receiving "cash and weapons, secretly trained guerrilla forces, [and] funded propaganda". Anti-communist activity in Afghanistan had already begun in 1979, but it "really swelled between 1981 and 1985". And, considering that the superpower worked through Saudi Arabia and Pakistan, it was no surprise that those picked to lead the fight were the "radical Islamist factions". Essentially, because it was so committed to defeating the USSR, the Reagan regime had no problem with acquiescing to Saudi and Pakistani tactics. Learning from the failure of Vietnam, US political elites had simply accepted that direct US intervention was not a good idea, and consequently **ignored warnings** that "many of America's favorite clients" in the Muslim World were actually "fundamentally anti-American in their outlook". In particular, Saudi Arabia and Pakistan funded Deobandis in Pashtunistan – the group ideologically closest to Wahhabism and which would eventually take power under the Taliban. Due to the fatal blow that would soon be dealt to the Soviet Union in the Afghan war, though, many US politicians would remain unrepentant about having fuelled the expansion of Wahhabi Islamism.

The USA's thoughtless, self-interested policy would inevitably have effects much further afield than Afghanistan. Osama bin Laden, for example, "began to... develop his global ambitions and his global organization" from the new Islamist safe-haven, receiving "indirect and sometimes direct support from the Pakistan army" in the process. As a result, Islamist militancy would soon spread to India, Yugoslavia, and Chechnya.

Nonetheless, Reagan's terminology of "noble freedom fighters" had managed to hide the complex political context of the Muslim World behind a simplistic (and erroneous) dichotomy of good versus evil until the World Trade Center attacks in 2001.[3]

Another partial result of imperialist interference in the Middle East was the **Iranian Revolution of 1979**, a mass uprising that found itself rooted in a context of the Western-backed coup of 1953, the West's consistent support for an oppressive monarch, and continued popular outrage at Israeli crimes against the Palestinian people. The rebellion, however, was unique, according to London School of Economics professor Fred Halliday, as it had not been led by a vanguard organisation, had received no foreign support, and had not been inspired primarily by secular radicalism. Instead, it had seen the locally-organised masses undertake a campaign of civil disobedience, protests, and strikes as part of a broad coalition to defeat both the monarchy and the country's imperialist-backed elites.

The revolution in Iran was independent, and that represented a danger to imperialist interests in the region, but it would soon lose much of the progressive impulse that had inspired it. For Iranian socialist Reza Fiyouzat, Antonio Gramsci's assertion that "a revolutionary situation simultaneously creates counter-revolutionary conditions" was proven correct by the corruption of the rebellion by Shia Islamists (who had actually helped to overthrow Mosaddegh back in 1953). The theocracy that would soon be installed, he argues, was "in fact the embodiment of imperialism in Iran", with clerics becoming "prolific at legislating... anti-labor laws" and asserting that their legitimacy did not come "from the people but from God".[4]

[3] http://www.democracynow.org/2004/6/10/ghost_wars_how_reagan_armed_the
[4] http://www.counterpunch.org/2014/10/24/the-iran-us-tango/

Nonetheless, US ally Saudi Arabia was worried about the Iranian clerics' anti-monarchical sentiments and their offer to lead the way in fighting against imperialism and Zionism in the Middle East. American elites, meanwhile, realised that it would be detrimental to their economic interests to have such a powerful player in regional politics adopt an anti-imperialist stance. Consequently, the imperial power began to forge a strategic alliance with the new leader of Iraq, **Saddam Hussein** (its former anti-progressive mercenary). After Hussein's invasion of Iran, the USA gradually sought to end its previous hostility towards the Iraqi Ba'athist regime, and would end up keeping quiet about the latter's numerous war crimes in order to further the cause of destroying independent governments in the region.

The new Shia Islamist regime in Iran, however, was actually strengthened by its resistance against Iraq, and managed to consolidate its power. The ongoing sectarian war in **Lebanon**, meanwhile, where Israel had been complicit in refugee camp massacres in 1982, created fertile ground for the growth in popularity of Iranian-inspired resistance movements – and the subsequent foundation of **Hezbollah** in 1985. In short, Iran and its allies were now at the forefront of anti-Zionist and anti-imperialist resistance in the Middle East (albeit with a reactionary ideology), and for that reason they were the forces that most worried the West and its regional proxies.

With the fall of the Soviet Union, and China having already opened up to capitalism, the world's economic elites were feeling understandably triumphant in the 1990s. For them, victory had been won, and the world's Left merely consisted of a few powerless hangers-on. The remaining independent nations in the world, meanwhile, could be coerced into changing through sanctions, international pressure, and covert interference. Not everyone fell so easily, however, and the return of the Republican Party to power in the United States in 2001 saw the start of **a more aggressive international strategy**. The threat of terrorism after the attacks of September 11 that year was a powerful enough rhetorical tool to give the ruling elites new licence to embark on hostile operations abroad, first in Afghanistan and then in Iraq. At the same time, the growing economic influence of China and the victory of Putin's nationalists in Russia gave powerful Americans even more of an excuse to **create a pro-imperialist foothold in the Middle East**, a resource-rich territory on the doorstep of the two independent superpowers.

However, the chaos created in the Middle East by the post-9/11 wars, the West's continuing support for repressive military regimes in the region, and the global capitalist crisis created unexpected consequences. Western allies began to feel intensifying pressure from protesters starting in late 2010, in what would soon become known as the **Arab Spring**. The West had to think quickly, and it responded with what Drake University professor Ismael Hossein-Zadeh called "**an all-out counterrevolutionary offensive**", which included: allowing some political figureheads to fall (whilst keeping the existing socio-economic order in place); supporting the suppression of protests elsewhere; claiming demonstrations were examples of sectarian conflict funded by Iran; or orchestrating what NSNBC's Dr Christof Lehmann referred to as "post-modern coup d'états".[5] One further reason for the failure of the Arab Spring to truly bring about profound change, however, was an apparent commitment of many citizens to liberal political reform. In other words, individuals came together without clear ideological proposals for societal transformation and simply expected enlightened elites to undertake a restructuring process 'from above'. In short, there was **no real**

---

[5] http://www.counterpunch.org/2012/04/13/whatever-happened-to-the-arab-spring/

project to place greater political and economic power into the hands of ordinary citizens.

While mass protests spread throughout the world after the Arab Spring, the Occupy Movement's talk of 'the 99%' encapsulated the anti-ideological nature of the uprisings, and thus the reason for their failure to present a real alternative. The apparent aim was to unite people from across the left and right against the corporate dictatorship which had become more apparent after the global capitalist crisis of 2007-8. This attempt at unity, however, was destined to fail because it sought to bring a wide range of ideologies together with no common strategy to change society. In other words, capitalism, nationalism, and theocratic rule still remained largely unchallenged throughout the world.

With the defeat of Gaddafi in Libya and the uprising against Assad in Syria, Western nations were once again supporting Islamist groupings, either directly or indirectly, in their quest to defeat unpredictable nationalist leaders. And, while they sought to install 'malleable' Islamists in power, their alliance with countries like Saudi Arabia, Qatar, and Turkey meant that they were almost destined not to get what they wanted. Having weakened secular and progressive movements in the region, supported Israel and military dictatorships, fostered sectarian chaos in Iraq, and nurtured reactionary Islamists for decades, the ground was ripe in the Muslim World for discriminatory and dogmatic extremists to put up the strongest resistance to the existing regimes. There was also a popular belief in many communities that the Quran did indeed hold "the germs for an alternative way of organising society", as Tariq Ali has noted.[6]

---

[6] https://www.greenleft.org.au/node/30057

Not all non-state Islamist organisations are the same
however, differing as they do in both kind and degree, and
each type would play a different role in the post-Arab Spring
Middle East. One group, for example, which had formed in
strong states and generally been forced into peaceful
participation in politics, gained its legitimacy without an
armed struggle, through doing work in communities like the
Muslim Brotherhood in Egypt. Another group, meanwhile,
gained its popularity and legitimacy primarily from its armed
resistance to the actions of aggressive neighbours (generally
Israel), though also through material support for the
communities from which they had sprung. These local
Islamists, which held certain nationalist tendencies, had
emerged in weak states (or non-states) and had proven
themselves to be among the best placed to protect their
populations from outside enemies. They would be
characterised mainly by Hezbollah in Lebanon and Hamas in
Gaza. The third type of organised Islamist, meanwhile, was
the 'takfiri' jihadi from a Wahhabi-inspired ideological
standpoint, who was not prepared to make concessions within
a political context and fully prepared to denounce fellow
Muslims as infidels. In short, they were radical,
discriminatory, and violent. And **ISIS** (which I will refer to as
Daesh from here onwards because of the negative
connotations this word has in Arabic), was the epitome of this
final category.

A significant number of Daesh fighters were **alienated or
radicalised Western Muslims**, with the foreign jihadi total in
Syria and Iraq exceeding 20,000 at the start of 2015 and thus
surpassing the number of foreigners who had participated in
the war in Afghanistan in the 1980s.[7] There was also talk of
former Iraqi Ba'ath Party members having joined the militant
group after having been excluded from the post-2003 military

---

[7] http://icsr.info/2015/01/foreign-fighter-total-syriairaq-now-exceeds-20000-surpasses-afghanistan-conflict-1980s/

structures in Iraq. What was very clear, however, was that Daesh's strong-armed approach and promises of change had convinced a number of Sunni citizens in a war-torn Syria and an increasingly sectarian Iraq to support it. In short, the chaos and division caused in Iraq by the 2003 invasion were now bearing fruits, as were the West's efforts to topple Assad in Syria by encouraging its allies in the region to support the regime's opponents. In particular, **Saudi Arabia and Qatar had been competing to fund the most effective Wahhabi jihadists in Syria**, with the former having purportedly created **Daesh** and the latter having funded **Jabhat al-Nusra** (the Syrian Al-Qaeda affiliate). And, with the local opposition having been weak from the very start, it very soon became clear that anyone who wanted to fight against Assad but didn't want to fight together with Daesh or al-Nusra would find their chances of success to be very slim.

Alongside massacring anyone who resisted their advances, happened not to be their kind of Muslim, or refused to submit to their rule, Daesh also took upon itself the task of killing educated women who criticised its rule and imprisoning women from other ethnic groups (like the Yezîdîs). Teenage girls would be among those who were kidnapped and taken away to be sold off as either the wives or sexual slaves of prominent jihadis. Its main focus, though, was "uprooting the toxic weeds", by which it meant non-Sunnis or Sunnis who questioned their extreme, violent, and discriminatory interpretation of Islam.[8]

To say that the USA and Western regimes in general were truly interested in fighting against Daesh, however, would be to ignore the fact that they had propped up regimes like that of Saudi Arabia for many decades without battering an eyelid. It would also be to ignore the role that the United States in

---

[8] http://www.memri.org/report/en/0/0/0/0/0/0/8157.htm

particular had played in nurturing Wahhabism in the first place and setting it free in Afghanistan in the 1980s. An analysis more in keeping with historical context, therefore, would be to suggest that the main reason the West would seek to destroy Daesh was that it wanted to avoid Syrian and Iraqi natural resources falling into the hands of a regime as hostile to Western interests (if not more so) as Assad. Another possible explanation as to why the West would suddenly care about Islamist presence in a region where it had long existed (thanks to its meddling) was that it was trying to repair the damage done in Syria by its Saudi, Qatari, and Turkish allies. Having given these regional powers free rein to throw everything they had at the Assad regime, the West now risked demands from its citizens that it stop supporting these state sponsors of terror. In short, the imperialist goal in Syria was to ensure the country's resources did not fall into the hands of an anti-imperialist opposition, and that its close allies were not put at risk in the process. The foolish and dogmatic actions of these regional associates, however, had meant it was almost necessary for the USA and its European colleagues to step up both their rhetoric and actions regarding the Syrian Civil War.

Having destroyed countries and killed countless civilians in previous interventions in the Muslim World, the West was finding it incredibly difficult to convince ordinary citizens that a bombing campaign in Syria was a good idea. The reason for this reality was perhaps that people were aware that the current situation was at least in part a direct result of previous military operations in the region. In other words, there were many people who understood that more bombs, more destruction, and more civilian deaths would be counterproductive, and would simply fuel the growth of Daesh and its violently rigid ideology even more. And even regional powers argued that the entrance of foreign ground forces would do infinitely more harm than good.

At the same time, the West's monster fabrication had proven in the past not to solve any problems in the Middle East (or elsewhere in the world). Instead, portraying enemies as irrational beings who had appeared spontaneously within a vacuum had simply perpetuated a cycle of ignorance, fear, hatred, and violence. To end the war in Syria, in short, there would have to be a long political process. First, all of the states prepared to sit around a table and negotiate a peaceful solution would need to be brought together. Secondly, for sustained peace, there would need to be an implementation of a meaningful system of democracy, along with freedom, equality, and justice. This route to ending the conflict would not be easy or perfect, and it would require the genuine political commitment of all of those involved, but it would be far better than a continuation of hostilities.[9]

---

[9] An in depth discussion of the links between imperialism and Islamism can be seen between Chapters 5 and 7 of *Rojava: An Alternative to Imperialism, Nationalism, and Islamism in the Middle East*

3) Syria, Turkey, and the Rojava Revolution

Independence isn't synonymous,
With revolutionary change,
And the errors of the past,
Needn't be the errors of today.

The outbreak of the Syrian Civil War saw the Left divided. Some immediately called for Assad to be overthrown; others called for him to be supported; and those who remained called for a more nuanced analysis of the situation. The reality is that Assad was a dictator, and the protests against him were justified. However, the West's aggression towards him was rooted in his independent stance, and the fact that he stood in the way of full Western control of Syria's natural resources. At the same time, Assad's regime was host to a significant number of Palestinian refugees, had a history of standing up to Israel, and was fighting for most of the civil war against an opposition that, in the most part, was reactionary. In other words, Assad was a tyrant, but he was a tyrant who had some progressive policies and who resisted imperialist aggression.

Whilst understanding the different sides of the argument, the question is 'do we really have to support one bastard or another?' Is everything in politics black and white? Is there always one side that is 'good' and another that is 'bad'? The answer to each of these questions is, of course, an emphatic 'no'. The reality is that just because someone is independent does not mean they are revolutionary. There are simply different types of anti-imperialist, ranging from incredibly reactionary to largely progressive. And the reality is that many of those in the world today, including Assad, unfortunately fall on the reactionary side of the scale.

The hostility of surrounding states in the Middle East towards Assad, however, was arguably more reactionary than the

Assad regime itself. Turkey in particular was ruled at the outbreak of the Syrian Civil War by an increasingly authoritarian character in **Recep Tayyip Erdoğan**, and by his neoliberal Islamist party known as the **AKP**. This party had arisen from a decades-long tradition of nationalist dictatorship, persecution of left-wing activists, and ethnic cleansing in Turkey, and it would have been incredibly surprising to see it make a break from that unfortunate tradition.

i) The PKK, the AKP, and Rojava

Contradicting conditions always,
Arise in complex contexts,
And while some feed profound changes,
Others see us repressed.

Within an atmosphere of increasing repression in the 1970s, left-wing activists began to favour a revolutionary solution, and began to organise themselves. Amidst the crackdown that followed the 1980 military coup, however, these progressives were forced into armed action sooner than they might have expected. Turkey's Kurdish communities would suffer perhaps more than any other in the country at this point, as they had for many decades previously, and the PKK stepped up to fight for radical societal change, but with a particular focus on Kurdish rights and freedoms. The Turkish State, though, had the second largest army in NATO, and was not about to let a Marxist rebel group make any gains. Although several thousand 'security' personnel were killed during this period, therefore, tens of thousands of suspected PKK militants and civilians were also murdered by the State. Many hundreds of thousands of people, meanwhile, found themselves displaced as a result of the violence and state repression.

In 1999, the worst of the fighting effectively ended when Turkish forces detained the PKK's leader, **Abdullah Öcalan**, with the help of the USA and the suspected support of Israel. Between Öcalan's arrest and 2004, ideological changes gradually took place within the PKK, as they had ever since the fall of the Soviet Union in 1991. Having announced a unilateral ceasefire, they sought to negotiate a peace settlement with the Turkish State, but found their petitions consistently ignored by Ankara. As a result of continued state repression and the government's reticence to take steps to resolve the Kurdish Question, fighting resumed between 2004 and late 2012. Again, the PKK sought to negotiate a political solution, but the AKP was not prepared to embark upon such a path.

With the PKK's Syrian affiliate (the **PYD**) pioneering the creation of an autonomous region in northern Syria (or 'Rojava') along with its progressive local allies, the cause of the PKK seemed to be gaining traction. Rojavan left-wingers, coming together in a coalition called **The Movement for a Democratic Society** (or **TEV-DEM**), stepped in to the vacuum left when the Syrian regime relocated most of its troops to other parts of Syria in 2012. The TEV-DEM and its defence militias (the YPG and later the female YPJ) took de facto control of the region and began to set in motion plans for a progressive libertarian administration, based on the twenty-first century ideology of the PKK.

Worried by events in Syria, Ankara sought to buy itself time by finally accepting the PKK's call for **peace negotiations** at the end of 2012. Its lack of action, however, along with its blockade and hostility towards the autonomous experiment in Rojava, showed that it was not truly committed to the process. It seemed that the move had more to do with the local elections in early 2014 and the first direct election of a president later in the year (in which Erdoğan would run).

With the party's difficulties in gaining support becoming apparent from the 2009 local elections and the 2011 general elections (when it lost, respectively, both municipalities and deputies), the peace process was almost certainly a political calculation based on attracted the support of conservative sectors of the country's Kurdish community.

The AKP regime had long shown itself to be in favour of state repression, whether of the press, social activism, or of its own former allies. Erdoğan's advocacy for greater presidential powers, meanwhile, gave rise to suggestions that he wanted to be the new Sultan of Turkey. He and others in his party had also expressed chauvinist views on a number of occasions. And, when Erdoğan became president in August 2014, the so-called 'solution process' with the PKK began to unravel. A month after his election, Daesh would launch an attack on the city of Kobanî in Rojava (which lay on the Turkish border), and Turkish forces would simply sit by and watch.

On a number of occasions, the Turkish State was accused of supporting Daesh, either directly or indirectly. After the outbreak of the Syrian Civil War, the country had effectively opened its doors to foreign jihadists, who would cross its borders into Islamist-held Syrian territory and train for war within Turkey itself. The AKP had clearly hoped to install an Islamist government of its own mould in Syria in the place of the nominally-secular Assad, and its significant support for fundamentalist rebels and hostility towards the Rojava Revolution seemed to be living proof of this aim.

At the same time, the PKK had shown itself to be a key player in the fight against Daesh in Iraq, while the YPG/YPJ had been successful at fighting against the jihadists in Rojava. Progressive Kurdish forces in both countries had stood up to Daesh with a fervour born from their secular, feminist, and democratic ideology, and were increasingly gaining attention and respect internationally for its protection of civilians and fierce anti-jihadi resistance. In short, they were the most broad-minded force in the Middle East, and the strongest ideological enemy of Daesh.

Nonetheless, the PKK's enemies, whether in Ankara or the KRG, sought to push forward myths about the group – based on questionable assertions about its past activities and an almost total ignorance of its currently stated principles. And, on the basis of these myths, they argued that the group deserved its place on the politically-motivated terror lists of the West, which had long included mostly independent movements while failing to include major terrorist sponsors like Western ally Saudi Arabia. The PKK itself, though, continued its battle to the death with Daesh, continued seeking a peaceful solution to the Kurdish Question in Turkey, and continued its support for the progressive system being built in Rojava, whilst outlining as clearly as possible its desire for a more democratic and inclusive Middle East.

ii) The Current Ideology of the PKK

We can't just oppose the bad,
We must fight for liberation,
Make proposals for a better world,
And democratic transformation.

The positive elements of the Rojava Revolution can be summarised in just one word: **equality**. The other elements, meanwhile, simply flow out from this term. In order to stop one sector of society oppressing another, for example, **autonomy** is key. If one party or one leader controls citizens or makes decisions for them, there will inevitably be ample opportunities for corruption and repression to take place. In other words, a true **direct democracy** (where all people have the power and freedom to make informed decisions about how to improve their lives) is absolutely essential for equality to exist. Furthermore, communities can only have greater economic justice if they are not subject to the exploitation of those in society who have material wealth. Therefore, the **cooperative organisation** of civilians must be strongly encouraged, and facilitated by **popular, democratic control over communal resources**.

At the same time, **women must no longer be subject to the whims of men and the chauvinist ideologies that they have too often defended**. They must have the power to make their own choices in life, and have an equal standing alongside men both in society and in the eyes of the law. And, finally, **citizens must be free to select the culture or religion to which they wish to adhere** without having any dogma imposed on them from above.

None of these ideas should appear particularly shocking to anyone coming from a progressive political tradition, but they are precisely the principles that the agents of imperialism have fought long and hard to destroy or obstruct. However, in the Rojava Revolution, these very ideas have emerged from the chaos created in Syria by imperialist proxies in the Middle East and Assad himself. Their proponents, then, made the most of a weak state in order to organise openly, forge an enlightened oasis of peace, and bravely defend themselves from heavily-armed reactionary opponents. And all of this arose from the **PKK's ideological transformation** which gained speed **after Öcalan's imprisonment in 1999**.

Originally, says Kurdish activist Ercan Ayboga, "the Kurdish freedom movement [in Turkey] had its ideological sources in the 1968 student movement and the Turkish left's Marxist-Leninist, Stalinist, Maoist, Trotskyist, and other communist theories". Then, however, "at the end of the 1980s", the PKK "embarked on a critique of the actually existing (state) socialist model". In the 1990s, this process of reflection led the group to focus increasingly on trying to change "individuals and society before taking the power of any state" and, in fact, on transforming the whole "relationship between individuals and [the] state". At this point, the movement decided that "a full democracy should be developed", in order to replace "big bureaucratic-technocratic structures", whether capitalist or 'communist'.

A big influence on this process was Öcalan, who "rejected the existing Marxist-Leninist structure" of the PKK after 1999 as "too hierarchical and not democratic enough". He soon began to foster a "political and civil struggle" which would replace the armed struggle "as the movement's center", promoting instead "civil disobedience and resistance" from 2000 onwards (with the Intifada in Palestine as an inspiration).[10]

In 2014, Rafael Taylor spoke at ROAR about how the PKK had transformed itself "into a force for radical democracy" in the early twenty-first century, and was "anything but narrowly nationalistic". Whilst in solitary confinement, he asserts, Öcalan had essentially adopted US 'social ecologist' Murray Bookchin's obscure form of socialism known as "libertarian municipalism". Having rebranded this vision as "democratic confederalism", the PKK leader Öcalan soon created the Union of Communities in Kurdistan (KCK), as the body for carrying out a "territorial experiment in a free and directly democratic society". And, although the international left-wing community was not aware of what was happening in this period, that did not mean it was not happening.

According to Taylor, there had been "a broader renaissance of libertarian leftist and independent literature... sweeping through the mountains" of Kurdistan since the collapse of the

---

[10] http://new-compass.net/article/kurdish-communalism

Soviet Union. During this period, Ayboga says, Kurdish leftists analysed "books and articles by philosophers, feminists, (neo-)anarchists, libertarian communists, communalists, and social ecologists". In prison, meanwhile, Öcalan was undertaking a "**thorough re-examination and self-criticism of the terrible violence, dogmatism, personality cult and authoritarianism**" that had been fostered during the PKK's war with Turkey. In fact, he would even say that his "**theory, programme and praxis of the 1970s produced nothing but futile separatism and violence**", insisting that: "the nationalism we should have opposed infested all of us". Nonetheless, Taylor argues, we should not forget the "authoritarian practices which sit ill beside [the PKK's] new libertarian rhetoric". At the same time, though, he asserts, when "**national liberation movements mimic the brutality of the state, it is invariably the unrepresented who are branded as the terrorists**" rather than the powerful elite establishment. In other words, the PKK's recognition of its past wrongdoings, together with its ideological change in course, demonstrated more political maturity than the repressive Turkish State has ever shown.

Finally a "free-thinker", Taylor suggests, **Öcalan had become "unshackled" from a dogmatic and inflexible "Marxist-Leninist mythology"**. Now, he asserts, the PKK's symbolic leader was now seeking not only an "alternative to capitalism", but also a "replacement for the collapsed model of … 'really existing socialism'". And, through the development of his "democratic confederalism", he drew inspiration from a number of "**communalist intellectuals, "movements like the Zapatistas", and other historical factors from the struggle in northern Kurdistan (Turkey)**". Essentially, the progressive Kurdish movement had now begun "actively internalizing the new philosophy" of "**eco-anarchism**" in both its "strategy and tactics", while "perusing **a largely non-violent strategy** aimed at greater regional autonomy".

After going to Turkey "to study the KCK on the ground", Bookchin's widow Janet Biehl shared her "interviews with Kurdish radicals involved in the day-to-day operations of the **democratic assemblies and federal structures**" on the New Compass website. She also translated and published "the first book-length anarchist study on the subject: Democratic Autonomy in North Kurdistan: The Council Movement, Gender Liberation, and Ecology (2013)". The PKK and KCK, Taylor claims, appeared to be "**following Bookchin's social ecology to the book**", including the "contradictory **participation in the state apparatus through elections**" of PKK allies that was "prescribed in the [Bookchinite] literature". Bookchin had effectively distinguished between "two ideas of politics, the Hellenic model and the Roman" (or "direct and representative democracy"), seeing his own vision as "**a practical revival of the ancient Athenian revolution**" (in the tradition of "**the Paris Commune** of 1871, the councils (soviets) in **the spring-time of the revolution in Russia** in 1917, and **the Spanish Revolution in 1936**").

The first of the five steps of Bookchin's communalism, says Taylor, consists of the **empowerment of** "existing **municipalities through law in an attempt to localize decision-making power**". The second, meanwhile, focusses on a **democratisation of those municipalities** "**through grassroots assemblies**". Then, the third seeks to **create a union of municipalities through** "regional networks and wider confederations... working to gradually replace nation-states with municipal confederations", with "'higher' levels of confederation [having] mainly coordinative and administrative functions".

The fourth step involves the **union of** "**progressive social movements**" in order to "**strengthen civil society and establish** "a common focal point for all citizens' initiatives and movements": **the assemblies"**. This cooperation would not expect that there would always be a "harmonious consensus", but would be built precisely out of the belief that "disagreement and deliberation" can be positive. For Bookchin, **"society develops through debate"**, though the assemblies would have to be secular so as to ensure the minimisation of "religious influences on politics and government" and that the focus remained on assemblies as an **"arena for class struggle"** rather than 'religious struggle'.

The final step Bookchin speaks of is the **"municipalization of the economy"**, which would contribute to the creation of a "classless society, based on **collective political control over the socially important means of production"**. There would also be a "confederal allocation of resources to ensure balance between regions", he says. In other words, there would be **"a combination of worker self-management and participatory planning** to meet social needs" in Bookchin's libertarian municipalism. In short, Taylor emphasises, this is all "classical anarchist economics".

Öcalan's democratic confederalism, meanwhile, placed emphasis on a **"democratic, ecological, gender-liberated society"**, and on a **"democracy without the state"**. For him, while "capitalist modernity" was based on "capitalism, the nation-state, and industrialism", his so-called **"democratic modernity"** would be based on a "democratic nation, communal economy, and ecological industry". In order to achieve the latter, he underlines, **"three projects"** would need to be undertaken: "one for the democratic republic, one for democratic-confederalism and one for democratic autonomy". As such, his pragmatic search for a "democratic republic" revealed (apart from a lack of reality-detached dogmatism) that he was looking to deal in a practical way with 'real world' conditions.

"Attaining long denied citizenship and civil rights for Kurds" in Turkey, for example, would be the project's main aim within the current state structures. Democratic autonomy and democratic confederalism, meanwhile, would seek to increase the "**autonomous capacities of people**", through building "a **more direct, less representative** form of political structure". For Wageningen University's Joost Jongerden and Ghent University's Ahmet Akkaya, this process would result in the creation of "a **bottom-up, participative administrative body, from local to provincial levels**" focussed on ensuring "basic civil liberties, such as the freedom of speech and organization", while the "core unit" of this model would be "**the neighborhood assembly**", otherwise known as "councils". These would then come together at the village, urban neighbourhood, district, city, and regional levels.

In Turkey, says Taylor, the councils set up by the KCK soon gained "popular participation" in a number of provinces, with Diyarbakır, "the largest city in Turkish Kurdistan", seeing assemblies spring up "almost everywhere". In the provinces of Hakkari and Sirnak, meanwhile, "two parallel authorities" were effectively created – one belonging to the KCK and one to the state (though "the democratic confederal structure [was] more powerful in practice").

Taylor then describes how "the "highest" level of federation in northern Kurdistan" was the **DTK (Democratic Society Congress)**, which was "**a mix of the rank-and-file** delegated by their peers [in the local councils] with recallable mandates" (60 percent) and "representatives from "more than **five hundred civil society organizations, labor unions, and political parties**" (40 percent). Of the latter, around six percent was "reserved for representatives of religious minorities, academics, or others with a particular expertise".

According to an "informal consensus among witnesses", he says: the "majority of decision-making [was] **directly democratic** through one arrangement or other"; the "**majority of those decisions [were] made at the grassroots**"; and "the decisions [were] executed from the bottom-up in accordance with the federal structure". As the assemblies and the DTK were "coordinated by the illegal KCK", however, "of which the PKK [was] a part", people involved in their activities consistently suffered repression at the hands of the Turkish State. One key element discouraging Turkish Kurds from participating in the PKK's directly democratic experiment, then, was almost certainly the fact that, upon doing so, they risked imprisonment or state persecution.

The DTK, as coordinated by the KCK, continued to move forward, however, and selected "the candidates of the pro-Kurdish BDP (Peace and Democracy Party) for the Turkish Parliament", which in turn proposed "democratic autonomy" for Turkey. [This party would soon be effectively replaced by the HDP, a coalition of Kurdish and Turkish progressives.] In essence, therefore, there was a "**combination of representative and direct democracy**" in the KCK's political model. Although it was seeking to work within the existing political system, however, the BDP would propose "the establishment of approximately 20 autonomous regions which would directly self-govern" issues of "education, health, culture, agriculture, industry, social services and security, women's issues, youth and sports". The state, in this scenario, would simply be left to conduct "foreign affairs, finance and defense". In short, whilst this proposal **did not represent a completely anti-statist stance**, such an achievement would undoubtedly be a significant step towards greater democracy and justice for Turkish citizens (and especially those in Kurdish communities).

"On the ground", however, "the revolution [had] already begun", with Turkish Kurdistan having already built up "an independent educational movement of "academies" that [held] discussion forums and seminars in neighborhoods". 'Culture Street', meanwhile, was a project which celebrated "the diversity of religions and belief systems" and restored mosques, synagogues, and Christian churches. There was also a campaign to put up municipality signs in both Kurdish and Turkish (a multilingual movement that gained the support of local shopkeepers).

Women's liberation, meanwhile, was being "pursued by the women themselves", with the DTK's Women's Council "enforcing new rules like the "forty percent gender quota" in the assemblies". At the same time, domestic violence was opposed by promising to give the salary of any abusive civil servant directly to his wife in order "to provide for her financial security and use as she [saw] fit". Elsewhere, in the fight against polygamy, "if a husband [took] a second wife, half of his estate [would go] to his first".

There were also "Peace Villages", which were "new or transformed communities of cooperatives", which implemented "their own program fully outside of the logistical constraints of the Kurdish-Turkish war". Along the Turkish border with Iraq and Iran, for example, ""several villages" joined the experiment". In another province, meanwhile, an "ecological women's village" was "being built to shelter victims of domestic violence" and supply them "with all or almost all the necessary energy".

At the same time, Taylor speaks about how the KCK would hold "biennial meetings in the mountains with hundreds of delegates" from KCK-affiliated parties in Turkey, Syria, Iran, and Iraq (including the PYD in Syria, PJAK in Iran, and the PCDK (Party for a Democratic Solution in Kurdistan) in Iraq –

all of which "promote democratic confederalism as well"). In the Qandil Mountains, meanwhile, Taylor stresses that "radical literature and assemblies thrive" among the PKK and PJAK guerrillas there, in an attempt to reintegrate "the mountains' many Kurds" into the model pioneered elsewhere in progressive Kurdistan "after decades of displacement".[11]

In September 2014, The Rojava Report gave a concrete example of how "certain villages in Colemêrg (Turkish: Hakkarı) [had] begun to found village communal assemblies in order to resolve their own problems". Residents in the village of Dizê (or Üzümcü), the site says, had begun "work on the formation of a village commune two years [previously]". The 735 inhabitants of the village, it asserts, would be "represented by two co-spokespersons – one man and one woman- who [would] change every year". Its "**Communal Assembly**", meanwhile, **would meet "twice a month with all residents of the village participating"**, in an attempt to "**determine the problems facing the village and develop projects to resolve them**". According to co-spokesperson Rıfat Er, the project had met with a lot of "excitement and enthusiasm", and was "based on developing relationships of communal living".

Having "received no services from the state... for a long time", The Rojava Report stresses, Dizê's inhabitants finally decided to "solve the problems facing [them] together", seeking to ensure that "everyone from the young to the old [could] take part in [assembly] meetings". As a result of "debate and common effort", it insists, they had now managed to build "village roads and... clean drinking water... fountains in common spaces". And, by basing their actions on "a system of duties developed by the village commune", they also took "care of road work and garbage collection". Essentially, there

[11] http://anarchistnews.org/content/new-pkk-unleashing-social-revolution-kurdistan and
http://roarmag.org/2014/08/pkk-kurdish-struggle-autonomy/

is no-one left without a task, and people only "contribute what they can for the commune". According to Er, the village's inhabitants believe their work "will lead to the founding of a truly democratic system where every village and district and city in our country will solve their problems through their own will".[12]

iii) The Parallel Process of the HDP

Peaceful change is ideal,
But they test our resolve,
When they cut off our paths,
And don't let us evolve.

Between 1990 and the present day, a number of progressive Kurdish parties were formed to overtly promote Kurdish cultural and political rights within the Turkish political system. The state, however, would ban and persecute the parties, claiming they were terrorist organisations. The European Court of Human Rights, for example, would be contacted by refugee Evrim Çiftçi in 2007, who claimed that, ten years previously, she had been "arrested and taken into police custody" for her activity in one of the parties, and the "police had obtained her confession by torture, in the form of suspension by her arms, beatings, insults and sexual assault". Eventually, the court would find that the applicant's "symptoms had [indeed] originated in treatment that had been inflicted on her during her time in police custody and for which Turkey bore responsibility".[13] And this example is just one from an incredibly long list.

For Baki Gul at KurdishQuestion.com, the aforementioned political parties were simply another element of the fight for progress which complemented "the struggle of the [PKK]

---

[12] http://rojavareport.wordpress.com/2014/09/01/village-communes-emerging-in-colemerg/
[13] http://insanhaklarimerkezi.bilgi.edu.tr/pages/news_full.asp?lid=en&id=149

guerrillas, the resistance of the prisoners of thought and the uprisings of the people". The 2008 formation of the BDP in particular, he says, finally brought "the democratic forces of Kurdistan and Turkey... together on a joint platform" – a project that had been attempted on previous occasions but had failed. This coalition, which "entered the general elections in 2011 [and] won a major victory", would essentially form "the foundation of the HDP project".[14]

In late 2011, the People's Democratic Congress (HDK) was established with the aim of uniting all left-wing movements in Turkey, including those seeking greater rights for Turkish Kurds. According to the BDP's Ertuðrul Kürkçü, the HDK sought to emphasise that "the reality of [a] pluralist society with [multiple] identities [would] be the most important opportunity to hinder the progress of mutual racism caused by war and conflict". This "multi-identity" reality, he said, was "Turkey's most precious treasure in [the] fight against racism". For him, "shoulder to shoulder with women, Kurds, laborers, those fighting for nature and life, youths, intellectuals, [and] workers", the HDK would "show that another Turkey is possible".[15]

Emre Uslu spoke at Today's Zaman in mid-2012 about how, since 2004, Abdullah Öcalan had been "arguing that pro-Kurdistan Workers' Party (PKK) parties should open their doors to Turkish politicians and free themselves from the Kurdish question". He suggests that Öcalan had "urged his lawyers to establish a new political party as an umbrella party to put Turkish socialists and Kurdish nationalist parties on the same political wavelength". In short, he had hoped that such a party would help to "reach out to the Turkish community to explain the Kurdish question" in a

[14] http://www.kurdishquestion.com/index.php/insight-research/analysis/bdp-for-an-autonomous-kurdistan-hdp-for-a-democratic-turkey/66-bdp-for-an-autonomous-kurdistan-hdp-for-a-democratic-turkey.html
[15] http://en.firatajans.com/news/hdk-becoming-a-political-party

more effective way. In other words, the hope was that the HDK could become a Turkey-wide version of the DTK (which was itself essentially the legal version of the KCK). "Both the HDK and the DTK", Uslu says, "were founded under the direction of Öcalan".[16]

PhD candidate Duygu Atlas, meanwhile, backs up this assertion, claiming that "the HDK was established at the behest of [Öcalan], as part of his plans to transform the Kurdish political movement into a 'party of Turkey' in order to become a legitimate political actor by shedding its ethnic-based politics" and including "a variety of minority groups, including Alevis, Armenians, Circassians, Laz, Arabs and Assyrians, as well as feminists, socialists, far-leftist parties, environmental movements, communities for the disabled, and lesbian and gay communities". Fundamentally, though, it was "a platform for the political unification of these underrepresented groups", which would materialise in 2012 with the creation of the HDP.[17]

The HDP, which "adopted the system of co-chairs [i.e. a man and woman sharing leadership roles] in line with its principle of equality at all levels", also showed its commitment to equality by allocating "a ten percent quota for LGBT individuals" in the party.[18] Furthermore, Atlas says, the HDP project "injected some new life into the heretofore feeble Turkish opposition", and this was partly thanks to the leadership of Öcalan.[19] HDP Co-chair Sebahat Tuncel, meanwhile, would insist that, with the PKK having sought

16 http://www.todayszaman.com/columnist/emre-uslu/the-pkks-turkish-initiative-hdk_280262.html
17 http://www.cftau.org/news-room/peoples-democracy-party-hdp-a-breath-of-fresh-air-for-the-turkish-opposition/
18 http://www.kurdishquestion.com/index.php/kurdistan/north-kurdistan/the-people-s-democracy-party-hdp-a-short-history/133-the-people-s-democracy-party-hdp-a-short-history.html
19 http://www.cftau.org/news-room/peoples-democracy-party-hdp-a-breath-of-fresh-air-for-the-turkish-opposition/

peace with the Turkish State, it was now 'the time of the HDP and HDK'.[20]

In 2012, Öcalan asserted that the PKK's aim was "not to separate the Kurds from Turks", and that its fight was instead "with the anti-democratism aimed at the Republic" from elite sectors of Turkish society.[21] In other words, he opposed the form of government within Turkey, but accepted that the destruction of the state itself was, at least for the time being, an unachievable goal. As a result, he claimed in March 2013 that the "era of armed struggle [had] come to an end" and that the struggle for Kurdish rights in Turkey would now "be advanced through political means".[22]

The Turkish government, however, failed "to take reciprocal confidence-building steps" after the PKK's initial withdrawal from Turkey, such as: the "release of at least 5,000 Kurdish activists from prisons"; the improvement of "Öcalan's conditions of incarceration"; the allowance of "mother-tongue education for the Kurds"; the reduction of "the 10% election threshold"; and the expansion of "the boundaries of freedoms of organizing, assembly and expressions". As a result, the "PKK military-political leadership" announced in early September that it "was suspending the withdrawal process".

Later the same month, Prime Minister Erdoğan reacted to the PKK's decision by unilaterally announcing a "democratization package", which would make certain reforms but would essentially change very little. For example, he granted Kurds the right to establish private schools for Kurdish language education, restored the names of Kurdish villages that had previously been changed into Turkish, gave Kurds the freedom to launch political campaigns in Kurdish, and

[20] http://www.diclehaber.com/en/news/content/view/407282?from=2910492152
[21] http://kurdishquestion.com/index.php/insight-research/abdullah-ocalan/the-republic-s-capitalist-modernity-project-and-emergence-of-the-pkk/89-the-republic-s-capitalist-modernity-project-and-emergence-of-the-pkk.html
[22] http://www.aljazeera.com/indepth/opinion/2013/05/2013514154722778273.html

abolished "the student's daily vow of allegiance that [started], "I am a Turk"".[23]

For Insight Turkey (IT), Erdoğan was simply trying to "maintain and even expand his electoral mandate" with the aforementioned measures, appeasing and satisfying "opposing constituencies" at the same time. By seeming too committed to the peace process with the PKK or conceding too many of the militants' demands, the organisation says, Erdoğan would have risked alienating other "elements of the electorate" which were "more important" to his party. Far from being dedicated to finding a solution to the country's military conflict, therefore, the Prime Minister seemed "to have treated the mere agreement to begin the peace process as the goal itself, rather than as a part of a process to address the root causes of the conflict". In short, IT asserts, the 'democratic package' of September 2013 had "failed to implement any of the reforms the Kurds were looking for".

In fact, the Turkish government was actually "constructing new military posts and dams, increasing the number of village guards, and failing to ensure the [negotiatory] connection between the PKK head Abdullah Öcalan and democratic circles". And, by taking these actions, the regime "was raising doubts about the peace process and creating the risk of a deadlock and failure".[24]

The subsequent social unrest in Turkey towards the end of 2014, meanwhile, was caused to some extent by the government's increasing authoritarianism, but also by its hostile stance towards Rojava and the besieged city of Kobanî. Nonetheless, the AKP sought to place blame the protests on 'subversive' PKK supporters and, in late October, Deputy Prime Minister Bülent Arınç even said: "from now on, we may

[23] http://www.al-monitor.com/pulse/originals/2013/11/akp-stall-kurd-peace-process.html#
[24] http://www.insightturkey.com/the-turkish-kurdish-peace-process-stalled-in-neutral/articles/1394

refrain from speaking about the resolution process" to which "we are not obliged".[25] In short, the government was apparently trying to use the 'solution process' as a restraining barrier on Kurdish protesters (to stop them from standing up against its internal repression and external hostility towards the Rojavan Revolution) and on the PKK (to stop it from returning to a state of all-out-war against the Turkish State). Essentially, then, it was testing the resolve of the progressive Kurdish movement as a whole.

Turkey's attempts to link Rojavan forces to the Assad regime in Syria, meanwhile, ignored the fact that the Ba'athist leader had rejected the idea of Kurdish autonomy (but simply could not do much to stop it from materialising as a result of his ferocious fight against opposition groups which were launching direct attacks on his forces). In fact, there would even be a number of intensified clashes between Rojavan and regime forces around the Cizîrê Canton (where the government still had control over the airport and border crossing of Qamişlo, along with a number of government buildings and Arab neighbourhoods in both Qamişlo and Hesîçe).

The HDP, though, would do its best to defend both the Rojava Revolution and the peace process, encouraging progressive Kurds to participate in non-violent protests and remain committed to a political solution. The party's fight, however, would be an uphill battle, with attacks being launched against it both physically and in most of the mainstream Turkish media. In short, it was becoming clearer and clearer that the AKP regime would do all it could to prevent the secular, left-wing movement in the country from gaining political ground.[26]

---

[25] http://www.hurriyetdailynews.com/turkish-govt-says-not-obliged-to-kurdish-peace-process.aspx?pageID=238&nID=73557&NewsCatID=338
[26] An in depth discussion of the Left's stance on the Syrian Civil War and the PKK's transformation in Turkey can be seen between Chapters 8 and 9 of *Rojava: An Alternative to Imperialism, Nationalism, and Islamism in the Middle East*

4) The Development of an Egalitarian Revolution

Ethnicity, religion, and gender,
Set aside so equality thrives,
Local councils empowering every street,
So humanity is revived.

In spite of hostility from Turkey and the Kurdish nationalist regime in northern Iraq, the libertarian left-wing experience in Rojava continued to take shape. According to Sabanci University's Yasin Duman, the Rojava Revolution's assertion of popular control over the "important oil resources" and "fertile lands" of the largely-Kurdish parts of northern Syria in 2012 had created **"an important change in power relations"** in the country. It had also given Kurds a stronger position than they had ever had in the past.

Although the progressive Kurdish movement "never refused dialogue with any party" inside or outside of Syria, it was nonetheless perceived by other groups in Syria and elsewhere to be more dangerous than ever before (as far as the latter's own interests were concerned). Therefore, it was left largely without allies (apart from the PKK) until 2014, fighting against "the FSA, Jabhat al-Nusra, the ISIS and Assad Forces since the beginning of the conflict". Only in February 2013 would the FSA and YPG sign an agreement "to defend some regions together and not attack each other" elsewhere.

While a division of the "multi-ethnic and multi-religious" Syria ("into three states: an Alawite state in the west, a Kurdish state in the north and a secular or Islamic Arab state… in the remaining parts of Syria") would perhaps seem like the most obvious solution to the civil war, Rojavan forces had made it very clear from the start that they did not seek secession from Syria but instead demanded **"a democratic and federal Syria** where Kurds and other ethnic and religious minorities [could] enjoy their rights". In fact, one manifestation of this policy was the attempts by the Autonomous Cantons of Rojava "to involve all... groups" in their attempts to "re-structure the society", and thus prevent Rojava from being turned into yet another battlefield. And, in precisely this way, they managed to remain "relatively calm and stable" until the intensified Daesh attacks in 2014.

In spite of the progressive, democratic aims of the Rojava Revolution, however, along with its determination to avoid the "creation of new conflicts" and its focus on the protection of human rights, the autonomous parts of northern Syria were subjected to "a harsh embargo" from the very beginning by Turkey and the KRG (with the complicity of their US allies). As a result, it was only a combination of effective self-management and solidarity from Kurdish citizens abroad that helped Syrian Kurds to "meet basic needs" and "solve their problems on their own".

The big problem for Turkey and the KRG was that the Rojava Revolution was **an example of how the PKK's proposals of democratic autonomy could actually work on the ground** to end the oppression of the region's marginalised populations. In other words, it was a living alternative to the nationalist model proposed by the corrupt, self-interested government of Iraqi Kurdistan and to the Turkish State's model of passing down minor, superficial changes from above. It also definitively placed into the Middle Eastern political debate the idea that "a community [could] get its freedom only if the women in that community [also became] free", by showing in Rojava how women, who experienced "**equal representation in all institutions**", had played such "an important role" in the construction of democratic autonomy. In short, Duman argues, success for the Rojava Revolution presented the risk of helping to "change the whole system in Turkey, Iraq and Iran, too".[27]

In short, the Rojavan cantons of Cizîrê (or Jazira), Kobanî (or Kobanê), and Efrîn (or Afrin) had all responded quickly to the so-called 'Arab Spring', and the "strong and effective" protests in these communities had "caused the withdrawal of the Syrian army".[28] This process had been different from that which had led to Kurdish autonomy in northern Iraq, however, where nationalists had forged both a long-standing alliance with the USA and a conservative bourgeois regime (i.e. a small, self-interested elite which claimed it would lead the fight for justice and independence). For this reason, argues Jerome Roos at ROAR, it is "very important to make a proper distinction between the nationalist-conservative government" in the KRG and "the libertarian-socialist experiments of the new PKK [and its allies] in Syria".

ROAR's Rafael Taylor, meanwhile, speaks about how "local councils popped up everywhere" after the dawn of Rojavan autonomy, and "self-defense committees were [soon] improvised". At the same time, Kurdish-language schools were established, "councils intervened in the equitable distribution of bread and gasoline", and women were "now free to unveil", being "strongly encouraged to participate in social life" as "old feudal ties" were being cut. Rojava's inhabitants were now "free to follow any or no religion", and the new system helped to build on the PKK's groundwork elsewhere to create the possibility of a "profound explosion of revolutionary culture and values" in the Middle East.[29] In fact, even Foreign Policy spoke in late 2012 about how

[27] http://kurdishquestion.com/kurdistan/west-kurdistan/syrian-civil-war-emergence-of-a-kurdish-autonomy-in-rojava/126-syrian-civil-war-emergence-of-a-kurdish-autonomy-in-rojava.html
[28] http://libcom.org/news/experiment-west-kurdistan-syrian-kurdistan-has-proved-people-can-make-changes-zaher-baher-2 and http://www.anarkismo.net/article/27301
[29] http://anarchistnews.org/content/new-pkk-unleashing-social-revolution-kurdistan and http://roarmag.org/2014/08/pkk-kurdish-struggle-autonomy/

"cultural centers [were blossoming] and new courts and local councils [were opening]" in Derik (in north-eastern Rojava).[30]

At the end of June, 2012, the PYD-led "revolutionary leftist coalition" of TEV-DEM officially embraced "the project of democratic autonomy and democratic confederalism as a possible model for Syria", and "hundreds of KCK (including PKK) fighters from across Kurdistan [crossed] the border to defend Rojava" from outside threats. In response, Turkey "threatened to invade Kurdish territories" in Syria, and the PYD suspected that **Turkey was** "**already engaged in a proxy war** against them **by facilitating the travel of international jihadists across the border to fight alongside the Islamists**" in the Syrian Civil War.

For Taylor, the progressive struggle of the PKK and its allies could now "form a silver lining in the dark clouds gathering over the Islamic State and the bloody inter-fascist wars between Islamism, Ba'athism and [the] religious sectarianism that gave birth to it". In his opinion, they were now "**defending radical democratic values with their lives**", and deserved the gratitude of all of those who valued "the idea of civilization".[31]

In **October 2013**, Glen Johnson spoke at VICE about how the **YPG/YPJ militias in Rojava had** "**battled al-Qaeda-linked militants... for much of the [previous] year**" (without receiving almost any mention in the international media). Daesh, Jabhat al-Nusra, and FSA militants, he says, had all been fighting in particular for "control of the oil-producing province" of Hesîçe. What was perhaps more striking, however, was "the **active participation of a large number of female fighters**" in the Rojavan defence forces, and women's presence in both the "**community-driven police force**"

[30] http://foreignpolicy.com/2012/10/25/the-war-for-free-kurdistan/
[31] http://roarmag.org/2014/08/pkk-kurdish-struggle-autonomy/

(Asayish) and in political structures. According to one female fighter, he asserts, "most Kurdish women [had stayed] in their homes... before the revolution" but, ever since, such "attitudes [had] been changing".

From the very start of the Rojava Revolution, Johnson notes, Islamist forces had sought to take control of northern Syria because of its "shared border with Turkey and Iraq". In particular, "al-Qaeda-linked fighters" had launched an early siege on Serêkanîye (Ras al-Ayn), which was, along with other parts of Rojava, of "strategic value" for the "smuggling and trafficking operations" of such jihadi groups. As a result of these aggressive attacks, Johnson reports, an "estimated 50,000 Kurds" had fled from Syria into Iraqi Kurdistan "in August [2013] alone".

In other words, although Rojavans had "largely avoided being drawn into the country's civil war", the constant Islamist attacks (along with the fact that "the Turkish government [had] allowed – by removing landmines and razor wire – ISIS and JN fighters to enter Ras al-Ayn from Turkish territory to assault YPG positions" there) were now drawing the YPG/YPJ further and further into the conflict.[32] The assault on Kobanî the following year would simply be a continuation and amplification of this struggle.

For Doctor Saladdin Ahmed, writing in May 2014, the progressive movement of Syrian Kurds had been "**dismissed not only by Western powers, but also by the Kurdistan Regional Government of Iraq**" and the international mainstream press since 2012 primarily **because of the PYD's key role in the Rojava Revolution**. In short, the group's ideology did not fit into the 'oppress or divide' mentality of imperialism in the Middle East, although at the same time it

---

[32] http://www.vice.com/read/meet-the-kurdish-female-freedom-fighters-of-syria @GlenAJohnson

did not express the type of "popular anti-western sentiment" that other imperialist foes in the region did (in spite of its clear opposition to imperialism and capitalism).

Nonetheless, Ahmed asserts, Kurds in Rojava had been **"singlehandedly resisting Islamist fundamentalists"** in Syria, who had grown in power thanks to foreign interference and who, ironically, were actually helpful to the Assad regime (which hoped to portray the opposition's uprising as a largely "jihadist campaign"). At the same time, though, Rojava was not enjoying any "material or symbolic support" from elsewhere in the world "on sectarian bases" (unlike the Alawite or Sunni areas of Syria).

For Ahmed, a key element of the Rojava experiment was the way in which "**Kurdish women [were] leading a revolutionary movement of social liberation from entrenched patriarchy**". In the Efrîn canton, for example, an "Alevi Kurdish woman named Hevi Ibrahim" had risen to be the prime minister. In fact, he asserts, Rojava is "**the only region in the world where women have organized themselves to ideologically and physically fight Islamist forces to protect civilians from fanatic religious rule**". And, in the process, he stresses, they were "transforming the entire society of Rojava and setting an inspiring example for the rest of the Islamic world, and wherever women [were] oppressed".

At the same time, he adds, there was also **ethnic and religious inclusiveness in Rojava**, and "minorities [had] joined Kurds in civic activities in the cantons as well as in the new administrations". In the Cizîrê Canton, for example, "the co-vice presidents [were] an Assyrian Christian woman and an Arab man". Finally, however, Ahmed criticises the "**humanitarian and economic embargo... imposed on Rojava**", asserting that, from a "secular, feminist, humanist, and humanitarian point view…, Rojava [deserved] international support and protection".[33]

i) Rojava's Focus on Women's Liberation

In August 2014, KurdishInfo.com also spoke about how women had **"played a key role** in the defence of [the city of] Kobanî" and had been **"demolishing taboos based on male domination"** ever since the Rojava Revolution began. Insisting that the YPJ is a "source of freedom", the site quotes one female militant as saying that, before joining the defence of Rojava, her life had been "between 4 walls", and she had "had no social or economic life". In the past, she asserted, she "never used to believe a woman could be the equal of a man". **In the YPJ,** however, she and her cousin **learnt that "male domination was not a normal part of life but was… against the natural order"**.

Berfin, meanwhile, joined the YPJ when ISIS attacks on Kobanî began to intensify in 2014. "Before joining the YPJ", she stresses, "we experienced serious assimilation". Being previously "alienated from our language and our culture by the regime which imposed Arab culture", she affirms, "here I have become acquainted with my own language and culture". In short, **the group changed her old perception that "women [were] lacking and [could not] do anything"**. Without the revolution, she insists, she would "probably have got married and been a child mother". At the same time, YPJ fighter Roza claims: "the most important gain of this conflict has been, in my opinion, the **breaking of feudal value judgments** in Kobanî".[34]

According to TEV-DEM head of diplomacy Chenna Saleh, the Rojavan administration believed that **politics was "one of the**

---

[33] http://www.yourmiddleeast.com/opinion/10-things-you-must-know-about-kurds-from-the-other-syria_23527
[34] http://www.kurdishinfo.com/ypj-fighters-demolishing-taboos

duties of a society" rather than "just the duty of a government", and that **citizens therefore had to make steps forward regarding women's liberation themselves.** While "many women [had been] joining the YPG and... playing a big role in the political struggle", one local human rights worker said, it was still **necessary to bring about "a change in the classic family structure"** in order for such advances in female participation to expand.[35]

Henife Husen, a member on the coordinating body of the women's Star Union Organisation (or Yekitiya Star), spoke in early March 2014 about how Abdullah Öcalan had told female followers that "the emergence of women's free will and a free women" would lead to "the emergence of a free society", and that such a society would subsequently lead to a "liberated humanity and nature". **Truly free women,** she insists, **remove themselves "from the status of property"** and take "natural morality as the [main] principal" in their lives. In Rojava, she says, the women's movement was developing a focus on the science of *jineology* (women's studies in Kurdish), and the Yekitiya Star was supporting **"the formation of free women's organizations"** throughout the region.

While "thousands of women [had] received education" in Rojavan academies about jineology and their rights, Husen asserts, "work around cooperatives [had also] started in order to include women". Rather than being firmly against all religion, she says, "we have taken the cultural dimension of the religion of Islam as our base but not its political dimension". In other words, she and her comrades were aware of the **"curse [that] the political dimension of religions [had represented] for humanity",** and that extremists like ISIS militants were just an example of that. Nonetheless, she stresses, many Arab women had "accepted the slavery of

[35] http://www.theage.com.au/world/kurds-unite-to-build-kurdistan-in-defiance-of-islamic-state-20150314-141xwp.html

women as a form of worship", and therefore had "no serious organization". And, although Kurdish and Syriac women had been "decisive in the formation of the cantons", they were also seeking to encourage greater female organisation within Arab communities in Rojava.[36]

In fact, Hediya Ali Yousif of the Star Union Organisation asserted that "the need for women to organize was crucial in order to collectively voice [their] rights and to claim [their] rightful place in society". In order to achieve these aims, she said, her group had "nurtured and utilized the newly won rights of congregation in Western Kurdistan to organize", to educate women, and to educate society as a whole, seeking mostly to "gain recognition [for women] as equal members at home and active participants of society". Formed "by feminist movements that [had] decided to join efforts and come together in order to gain and protect the rights of women", she stressed, the group was at the forefront of the Rojava Revolution.[37]

In October 2014, University of Cambridge PhD student and Kurdish activist Dilar Dirik spoke to Asheville FM's 'The Final Straw' about how the "PYD [had] been attempting to create a dual power situation" in northern Syria, based on an "anti-state, anti-capitalist, feminist & ecological critique". As a Kurdish refugee herself, Dirik emphasises how "a series of communes, councils and alternative representational structures" had been set up since the PYD and its allies took the reins of the three independent cantons of Rojava in 2012. She also refers to "the methodologies of the Kurdish Women's movement in Rojava to autonomously push the PYD… to center on gender balance in all functions, moving to shift

[36] https://rojavareport.wordpress.com/2014/03/07/women-will-not-leave-their-freedom-for-after-the-revolution/
[37] http://www.kurdishinstitute.be/star-union-organization/

things often called "women's issues" to the fore and make them issues for the movement at large".

Dirik reaffirms that the PYD is part of the PKK-led shift in the Kurdish movement which focusses on the "**embracing of a stateless status** and an attempt to invite and include as many ethnic, religious and national communities and individuals of the region into the implementation of Democratic Confederalism" as possible. The Final Straw suggests that the US public probably hadn't heard of Rojava before "because it [challenged] the stability of U.S. allies like Turkey" in the Middle East, and because it teased "the boundaries between philosophies" seldom spoken about in American society whilst attempting to "put them into practice".[38]

ii) Rojava's Fight for Secular Unity

Although Syriacs had initially hoped to stay out of the Syrian Civil War, the increasing violence led some to support Assad's regime. However, the Syriac Union Party soon decided to work alongside the PYD, thus increasing Syriac representation in Rojava's cantons. In fact, according to the European Syriac Union (ESU), the region's democratic autonomy "increased the moral of our people".[39] Syriac Orthodox Priest Şemun Demir, meanwhile, who lives in Germany, insists that "**when religion becomes a part of politics it opens the way to disaster**". Because Syriacs had previously "shared the same fate" of oppression, he says, "we look at Kurds as being closer to us". The struggle of Kurds in Rojava, for Demir, was "**in the service [of] humanity**", and he emphasises that Syriacs and Kurds could "live [together] as brothers in line with the philosophy of Abdullah Öcalan".[40]

---

[38] http://www.ashevillefm.org/the-final-straw/10/2014/dilar-dirik-on-the-rojava-revolution-part-1 and http://dilar91.blogspot.com/
[39] http://rojavareport.wordpress.com/2014/04/21/european-syriac-union-democratic-autonomy-has-increased-the-moral-of-our-people/
[40] http://rojavareport.wordpress.com/2013/10/17/syriac-priest-let-us-build-a-life-around-ocalans-philosophy/

In August 2014, a Syriac fighter from Derik in the Cizîrê Canton of Rojava spoke about how she had joined the fight to save the Rojava Revolution in 2012. Having been raised in Damascus, Sena İbrahim (also known as Zin Zagros) says that, after the outbreak of the civil war, it became "impossible for Syriacs to live in much of the country". As a result of "large-scale massacres", she asserts, she and her family soon "moved to Rojava", where **the system of democratic autonomy made it "possible for all segments of society to live a free life"**.

Many local Christians, she stresses, initially viewed the Rojava Revolution "with scepticism", but "**Armenians and Syriacs [soon] came to understand that they had a place in this order**", and thus "began to take part in the administration of the cantons and locally autonomous governments". It was **a system "in which people accepted one another and showed respect for one another whatever one's cultural or religious background"**, and in which the seeds of a "**culture of a common life**" had been sown. Furthermore, when it became clear that Wahhabi attacks on Rojava "were entirely targeted against Syriacs, Armenians and Kurds", these communities "realized [more than ever] **the need for a life of cooperation and stronger organization**". In short, Zagros says, "there is [now] no need, as in the past, to go and introduce someone to the [ideology of the] PKK", because people can "see these realities with their own eyes", and they know exactly what the PKK and its allies stand for.[41]

According to Yasin Duman, meanwhile, "Kurds and Assyrians in [the] Cizîrê Canton" both believed that the attendees of the **Geneva I and Geneva II conferences** (which were supposedly aimed at finding a solution to the Syrian Civil War) had not been "representatives of the people" but

[41] http://rojavareport.wordpress.com/2014/08/12/syriac-guerilla-now-is-the-time-to-join-the-revolution/ and http://www.diclehaber.com/en/news/content/view/414970?from=3534286294

rather "sought interests of international and regional states and powers". For that reason, he says, these communities were not surprised that the meetings failed to "find a political resolution" to the Syrian conflict. In Rojava, however, **the TEV-DEM had proposed an alternative to these conferences by declaring the democratic autonomy of Rojava's three cantons in January 2014.** Essentially, then, the absence of a progressive presence in the Geneva conferences had led the PYD and its allies in Syrian Kurdistan to take matters into their own hands.

The Rojava Revolution, Duman asserts, "**does not promote the superiority of any single ethnic or religious identity**", and therefore seeks to include all groups in order to emphasise that **responsibility for governing the region "is shared"** and to ensure that "cooperation among the groups increases". As a result of this philosophy, he affirms, "the people of Rojava (around 80%) support and own the revolution", with a significant part of the "remaining 20%" feeling reluctant primarily because of fears that Assad's forces would eventually return and seek vengeance on those who had been involved in the revolutionary process. (A smaller number, meanwhile, simply wanted "to live their identity and social status as it was before, superior to minorities".) The aforementioned fears, Duman insists, are likely to be "overcome in time", though **"nationalistic ideas" which "do not accept the equality of ethnic and religious identities" are those "with which democratic autonomy [will have] to struggle the most"**.[42]

Rojavan autonomy, asserts Alastair Stephens at Counterfire, was not spoken about in the mainstream media primarily because it **did not "fit the narrative... being developed... by forces both inside and outside the country"**. These news

[42] http://kurdishquestion.com/insight-research/analysis/rojava-unity-in-diversity/214-rojava-unity-in-diversity.html

outlets, he says, guided largely by the stance of their respective governments, focussed primarily on a fight between different sects, speaking mainly of the struggle between an orthodox Sunni population and the unorthodox Alawis in Assad's government (along with the Druze and Christian minorities which were collaborating with them). Syria's Kurds, however, with around 2.5 million people and representing roughly 10% of the population, were in reality "the largest minority group in the country" in spite of their Sunni faith, primarily because they were not Arabs. Furthermore, due to the "common Kurmanji language" they shared with Turkish Kurds (along with the historic presence of the PKK in Syria) had meant they had been more influenced by the progressive Kurdish movement of Turkey than by the reactionary nationalist movements of Iraq and Iran. As a result, their ideas would be likely to clash with whoever ended up with power in Damascus.

The Free Syrian Army, for example, stated that it would "not allow the formation of federal regions in Syria" – a unified petition made by the majority of the country's Kurds. Consequently, the main Kurdish groups in Rojava chose not to participate in the Turkish-backed Syrian National Council (SNC) - "the main umbrella group bringing together [pro-Western/capitalist] exile leaders". And, although some individual Kurds (who had lived in exile and enjoyed few links with Kurdish parties within Syria) did indeed participate in the SNC, they did not represent the will of the majority of inhabitants in Syrian Kurdistan.

Another reason for the Syrian Kurds' refusal to participate in the SNC, meanwhile, was because of the latter's links to Turkey, which one Syrian Kurdish party leader asserted was "against the Kurds… in all parts of the world". He continued, saying: "**if Turkey doesn't give rights to its 25 million Kurds, how can it defend the rights of [Syrian Kurds]?**" In short, by distancing themselves from the mainstream, Western-backed opposition, therefore, Rojava's Kurds were aiming to avoid becoming "tied into alliances with forces which could turn on them later". The departure of Assad's regime from Rojava in 2012, therefore, could possibly have been a result of the Ba'athists' perception that, because Rojavan parties were not allying themselves with the mainstream opposition, they posed less of a danger to the government in Damascus. At the same time, said one PYD leader, it was necessary to have "a de facto truce between the Kurds and the government" at the moment of the revolution because, simply speaking, the PYD's militias were not yet strong enough to compete with a well-funded army, and it would have been incredibly difficult to set up autonomous organisations and committees in the middle of an all-out war with the state.[43] In other words, the PYD and its allies could not afford to get stuck in a quagmire of armed conflict, especially considering the incredibly limited support they received at the time from the outside world.

In July 2014, Toronto-based activist and PhD student Sardar Saadi argued that the Rojava Revolution was an incredibly revolutionary experience, especially considering how marginalised left-wing groups in the Middle East had become as a result of imperialist policies during the Cold War – when the West undermined "radical student groups, feminist organizations, national liberation and anti-colonial struggles, labor and peasant movements, and leftist intellectuals". These movements, Saadi asserts, were precisely the forces on "the front-line of struggle against authoritarian regimes, regressive religious beliefs, and imperialist powers' domination in the region", but the context of their debilitation at the hands of imperialists would nonetheless be totally ignored by the "mainstream media's coverage" of the "brutal advance" of

---

[43] http://www.counterfire.org/index.php/articles/international/16052-the-kurdish-question-in-syria-a-lithmus-test

Daesh. These outlets, he says, simply did "not bother to look at the role of their governments in the current chaos".

The imperialist strategy during the twentieth century, Saadi explains, resulted in a "massive wave of oppression, arrest and slaughter of leftist activists and intellectuals", especially in the 70s and 80s, and these actions "had irreversible effects on the social dynamics and movements in the region". As leftists were repressed, imprisoned, or exiled, he insists, "jihadist groups started to rise because of the major support they received from Western powers in the role of proxy organizations". As part of an imperialist strategy determined to "erase all traces of the political left in the region", these militants subsequently "started to grow like cancer cells in every corner of the region" as soon as they had finished "silencing the left". After the West's twenty-first-century invasions, meanwhile, these organisations even "gained a legitimate presence and status" in the region, as they were seen as effective military resistance to "foreign invaders".

Meanwhile, the West propped up supposedly "moderate" Islamists which effectively worked as "agents of global capital in the region". The increasing "power and confidence" of the AKP in Turkey, however, was a perfect illustration of how this tactic essentially "brought [even] more devastation and sectarian violence between Shias and Sunnis" to the region. In Syria, for example, the Turkish government actually "played a key role in worsening the situation", by allowing its borders to function as a "transit location for extreme Islamists from all around the world on their way" to the country. Furthermore, on top of providing a "safe haven for (aspiring) jihadists", Turkey was also criticised for giving them "logistical and military support" (with both Daesh and the Al-Nusra Front being thought to have benefitted from Turkish aid).

For Saadi, the so-called "moderate" Islamist agenda in Turkey had been successful in defending neoliberalism, cracking down on "secular and leftist opposition" in the 2013 Gezi protests, and fuelling reactionary Islamism. In other words, the jihadist groups in Syria were simply "one part of a larger problem", which included both the counter-revolutionary "violence and suppression of authoritarian regimes and imperialist rule" in general.

The Rojava Revolution, however, would be a genuine, long-lasting solution to reactionary Islamism, according to Saadi. Having "shown their ability and willingness" to build a path forward, he insists, the PYD and its allies finally announced in November 2013 "that they had finished all the preparations for declaring autonomy", and that they would subsequently propose "a constitution called the Charter of Social Contract". The goal of their system of democratic self-government, he asserts, was to form "**an alternative for all**", whilst intelligently (given their lack of resources) declaring "that they would **only use their military forces to defend themselves**".

Meanwhile, Saadi asserts, there were "many similarities" between the Zapatista experience in Mexico and the Rojava Revolution in Syria, particularly "in terms of their position in both regional and international affairs", such as: **the creation of autonomous government, popular assemblies, and gender equality; anti-imperialism and anti-authoritarianism; ecological preservation and respect for all living creatures; and self-defence.** Rojava's 'Charter of Social Contract', meanwhile, represented a "historic breakthrough", and was the "most democratic constitution" that people in the Middle East had ever had, as it claimed: "Kurds, Arabs, Assyrians (Assyrian Chaldeans, Arameans), Turkmen, Armenians, and Chechens, by [their] free will, announce this [autonomy] to ensure justice, freedom, democracy, and the rights of women and children in accordance with the principles of ecological balance, freedom of religions and beliefs, and equality without discrimination on the basis of race, religion, creed, doctrine or gender". In short, its aim was to facilitate the creation of a "democratic society" that would "function with **mutual understanding and coexistence within diversity and respect for the principle of self-determination and self-defence of the People"**.

More dangerously for the maintenance of nation states in the region, however, was the fact that the Charter claimed that Rojavans did "**not recognise the concept of a nation state... based on the grounds of military power, religion, and centralism**". In particular, such a belief could seriously threaten US economic hegemony in the Middle East, whilst dealing a significant blow to the governing elites of the region.

On a daily basis, says Saadi, the TEV-DEM was the body in Rojava "responsible for implementing [the above] principles" which, in spite of its ideology, recognised that **the path to an ideal society would be a long one and would take time to build** (especially in an environment of hostility from all sides). Overall, asserts Saadi, in seeking to **challenge the "oppressive rituals within religious communities**" and propose a "working pattern of co-existence with all the cultures and beliefs in the area, without violating the rights of any", Rojava could truly be the 'model to follow' in the Middle East. And the fact was, he emphasises, that it was not just a utopian dream on the horizon but a **real-world experiment that had "proved its viability through practical solutions and the everyday realization of the ideas presented in The Charter of Social Contract"**.[44]

ROAR Magazine's Ali Bektaş, meanwhile, echoes Saadi's call for solidarity with Rojava, emphasising how "thousands of

---

[44] http://roarmag.org/2014/07/rojava-autonomy-syrian-kurds/ and http://www.truth-out.org/news/item/25266-rojava-revolution-building-autonomy-in-the-middle-east

Kurds" had tried to "break down the Turkish-Syrian border" to join their besieged comrades in Kobanî in late 2014. This situation, he says, resembled other parts of the world where nation states had also tried to block free movement and separate populations with walls (like, for example, "the militarized wall between the US and Mexico" or "Israel's apartheid wall around the West Bank").[45] Having been arbitrarily separated after the fall of the Ottoman Empire and having suffered numerous massacres (such as the Dersim massacre of 1937-38, which saw up to 70,000 people killed), however, oppressed Kurdish communities were among the least likely to respect the rule imposed from above.[46] In short, with tens of thousands of Kurds having been killed in Turkey and "4,500 Kurdish villages [having been] evacuated and burnt by the Turkish military" during its crackdown against the PKK, the state had a very poor reputation among Kurds.

Since the PKK's reformation in the early twenty-first century, Bektaş explains, more emphasis now fell on the use of "legal political parties" and "different modes of civil disobedience" (such as the formation of groups focussed on local organisation) to **simultaneously bring about change from within the existing political system and from the grassroots.** Having had ample experience of arbitrary barriers, "the radical Kurds of Turkey and Syria" finally began to take "advantage of the geopolitical shake-up in the region" in the midst of the Syrian Civil War, and the Rojava Revolution aimed to set up a system of "self-governance with assemblies that [extended] down to the neighborhood level". In fact, the January 2014 Charter would guarantee "**decentralization, free education in the native tongue, healthcare, housing and an end to child labor and any discrimination against women**". And, to ensure the implementation of the latter point, "nearly all political organizations" formed in Rojava would "have **two**

[45] http://roarmag.org/2014/07/kurdistan-rojova-syria-autonomy/
[46] http://www.pen-kurd.org/almani/haydar/Dersim-PresseerklC3A4rungEnglish.pdf

leaders, one a man and another a woman". The "autonomous force" of the YPJ, meanwhile, would be "formed within the YPG" in April 2012 in order to make sure female fighters were held on an equal level to their male counterparts.

While the Western media had largely ignored the experiences of progressive Kurds since the Arab Spring, Daesh's capture of Mosul in June 2014 made it impossible to ignore the jihadist expansion in the region – which would soon shift focus more and more towards the anti-Daesh resistance of Rojava, coinciding in particular with the Islamists' "siege of Rojava's central canton of Kobanî" from July 2014 onwards (in which the jihadists would use "military equipment and munitions captured following their victory in Mosul"). Many Kurds in the region, meanwhile, believed that **Turkey was "using ISIS for a proxy war against Kurdish autonomy [in Rojava] by supplying them with arms and intelligence and free movement across its borders"**.[47] As a result, "Kurdish and Leftist political actors in Turkey" (mostly linked to the HDP) "mobilized to intervene in the situation", setting up "four different encampments along the border in strategic locations to prevent regular ISIS movements in and out of Turkey". These solidarity camps would also function as crossing points for Turkish Kurds wishing to join the anti-Daesh resistance of the YPG/YPJ in Kobanî.

Amidst a climate of **"wartime mobilization"** in Turkey, with "daily calls by party members for the youth to remove the borders and join the defense forces in Rojava", it was becoming increasingly difficult for the world's media to ignore what was going on in northern Syria (mainly because Turkey supposedly had a Western-style democracy), though they generally did their best to remain quiet. On the "second anniversary of the revolution in Rojava" (on July 18, 2014),

---

47 More on Turkey's collaboration and complicity with Daesh's attacks can be seen in Chapters 11 and 12 of *Rojava: An Alternative to Imperialism, Nationalism, and Islamism in the Middle East*

Bektaş notes, "thousands of Kurds flooded into the encampment in the township of Pîrsûs (Suruç in Turkish)" to "celebrate the revolution in Rojava and to remove the border so as to join their compatriots on the other side in their war against ISIS".

In turn, this movement soon attracted "more and more tanks and armored personal carriers of the Turkish military", along with "water canons and other armored vehicles of the police". Nonetheless, he asserts, the "Kurdish villagers and militant youth... remained determined to destroy this border between them and their comrades under siege". In a clear sign of increasing government authoritarianism, the celebration of the revolution was attacked with "hundreds of teargas canisters" and the crowd was assaulted "with batons and water cannons". And, although the activists resisted for two hours, police and soldiers "forced their way into the area with the tents and set fire to it all". At this point, it was clear to many activists that the Turkish government either wanted to help Daesh with its advance on Kobanî or to destroy the Rojava Revolution (which were basically the same thing).

While Turkey and the KRG sought to destabilise the Rojava Revolution, then, Turkish Kurds increasingly saw "the defense of Kobanî as... crucial... to keep the battle for Kurdish autonomy alive", comparing it to the "defense of the Spanish Revolution against the fascists in the late 1930s". In fact, Bektaş asserts, the "perseverance of the revolution in Rojava" was "the only remote hope for a different kind of Middle East, where peoples [could] come together in solidarity with each other rather than at war under sectarianism stoked by colonial powers".[48]

---

[48] http://roarmag.org/2014/07/kurdistan-rojova-syria-autonomy/ - contact the author at ali@riseup.net or follow @breakingkurd

iii) A Communal Revolution

In short, the PKK's project of democratic autonomy had now permanently replaced its previous independence struggle as a more viable option on the ground. University of Manchester PhD candidate Ulrike Flader, for example, describes the strong influence that Murray Bookchin's "decentralised, radical democracy **within or despite the given nation-states**" had played on the transformation of the progressive Kurdish movement. And this ideology could be seen clearly in Rojava, where certain elements of Ba'athist infrastructure had been quickly dismantled. **The education system and the legal system**, for example, had already been **transformed significantly.** The new system, meanwhile, had focussed primarily on: introducing "**direct self-government through communes**"; assuring "**equal participation in all areas of decision-making for all faith and ethnic groups**"; and strengthening "**the position of women**" in society.

For example, "**village or street communes**" had been set up with the aim of "**decentralizing decision-making** and realizing self-rule", and they had the power to determine how electricity and food would be administered, whilst also "discussing and solving other social problems". There were now "**commissions for the organisation of defence, justice, infrastructure, ecology, youth, as well as economy**", Flader says, and some "**communal cooperatives**" had also been created. The "poorest of the community", meanwhile, were supported with "basic nutrition and fuel".

Overall, Flader insists, each of the aforementioned communes assured that its own voice was heard by sending delegates to "a council for 7-10 villages or a city-district". Subsequently, she explains, the city councils are "made up of representatives of the communes, all political parties, the organisation of the fallen fighters, the women's organisation, and the youth organisation". At the same time, **each council has "a 40% quota for women"**, both "a female and male chairperson", and **decisions must be made by consensus**. The members of the councils, Flader says, are both "suggested and elected by the population".

Flader then quotes PYD co-chair Salih Muslim, who asserted that "this radical change from dictatorship to this form of self-rule [would not be] an easy process", and emphasised that the People were still "**learning how to govern themselves**". At the same time, however, a parallel legal system had already been in place in Syrian Kurdistan since the 1990s, albeit underground. These "peace and consensus committees" had been "developed as leftist Kurdish underground institutions", and had been "severely repressed in the 2000s". Since 2011, though, they had "resumed their importance".

The above committees, Flader explains, aimed to **deal with** "**all general legal questions and disputes** apart from severe crimes such as murder", in order to "**achieve a consensus between the conflicting parties**" which could lead to "a lasting settlement". In every commune, she says, "5-9 members" are elected to these committees, "according to their ability to facilitate such a consensus in discussion between the parties". In order to deal specifically with "crimes against women", meanwhile, there were now "**parallel women-only committees**", **which would attend to cases of** "**domestic violence, forced-marriages and multiple marriages**". If a consensus could not be found at the local level, however, the case would then move on "to higher institutions which exist on city, regional and canton level".

Regarding Rojava's **Social Contract**, meanwhile, Flader describes how it worked as a type of constitution, and how it was "**developed out of meetings among representatives of different ethnic and belief groups**". Its aim, she reports, is "**to** secure safety and self-rule to all groups", whilst ensuring their "right to organise themselves autonomously". And, although citizens in Rojava were "supported in participating in the... YPG", for example, they were also helped in the "founding [of] their own self-defence groups, as the Assyrians [had] done most recently".

According to PYD co-chair Asya Abdullah, Flader says, "the women's question [could not] be left until after the revolution", and was therefore something that the Rojava Revolution had sought to focus on. As a result of these efforts, she asserts, women in Rojava were "playing a leading role in politics, diplomacy, social questions", and "in the building of a new democratic family structure as well as in self-defence". In summary, Flader insists, Rojavans hoped that, by emphasising their "co-existence with the state, but on the premises of grassroots self-determination, pluralism and gender-equality", they could have "a peaceful democratic transformation" in their territories.[49]

[49] http://www.movements.manchester.ac.uk/the-alternative-in-syria/

5) Testimonies from the Ground[50]

A communal experiment unique in the world,
Seeking to reconcile,
A sad reality of xenophobes,
With a utopia of xenophiles.

The Rojava Revolution was not just a project dreamed up in the imagination of some left-wing academic somewhere in the West. It was a real-world experience witnessed both by the inhabitants of Rojava and by progressive sympathisers from abroad. **Zaher Baher** of the Haringey Solidarity Group, for example, spent two weeks in northern Syria in May 2014.

Baher speaks at LibCom.org of how he was given "**total freedom... to see and speak to whoever [he] wanted to**", including "women, men, youth, and the political parties" (of which there were over twenty in the region). He met, for example, "members of the different committees, local groups and communes" that had been set up, "as well as businesspeople, shopkeepers, workers, people in the market and people who were just walking in the street".

The TEV-DEM, Baher says, was formed "with the support of the PYD & PKK" with the aim of directing the region's revolutionary process, and had soon become "very strong and popular among the region's population". Essentially, he asserts, the group had stepped in "to implement its plans and programs" after the withdrawal of Assad's troops "before the situation became worse". Their programmes were not just spontaneous, however, and were "very inclusive" and comprehensive from the start. For example, **the organisation set up "a variety of groups, committees and communes on the streets in neighborhoods, villages, counties and small**

---

[50] An in depth discussion of the Rojava Revolution can be seen in Chapter 10 of *Rojava: An Alternative to Imperialism, Nationalism, and Islamism in the Middle East*

and big towns everywhere". The aim was to involve all citizens in resolving problems and making decisions that would affect them. After a short time, Baher reports, these committees had begun to meet every week, and had their own representatives "in the main group in the villages or towns called the "House of the People"".

In his experience, Baher asserts, the TEV-DEM was "the most successful organ in [Rojavan] society", and its participants were capable of achieving "all the tasks they [had] been set". He justifies his opinion by explaining how the group was determined, hopeful, and **committed to "working voluntarily at all levels of service to make the event/experiment successful"**. He also speaks about how it had been instrumental in setting up the YPG/YPJ (as a common Rojavan self-defence force) and the "Asaish (a mixed force of men and women that [existed] in the towns and all the checkpoints outside the towns to protect civilians from any external threat)". There was also **a special police unit**, he says, which was **"for women only, to deal with issues of rape and domestic violence"**.

Unlike protesters during the Arab Spring (who as a general rule hoped change would come from above – whether from a political class, a religious class, or a military class), Baher asserts, most Rojavans "were prepared and knew what they wanted" when they suddenly found themselves in the unprecedented position of being able to govern themselves in 2012. In short, they wanted a revolution that would "start from the bottom of society and not from the top", and one that would be fundamentally "against the state, power and authority". A central part of this project, then, would be aimed at **giving all civilians "the final decision-making responsibilities"**.

According to Baher, "a lot of hard work, discussions and thought" went into the TEV-DEM's decision that a Democratic Self Administration (DSA) was needed to govern the Rojavan cantons of Cizîrê, Kobanî, and Efrîn. As a result, the "People's Assembly elected their own DSA" in mid-January 2014, which had the autonomy to "implement and execute the decisions" of the main TEV-DEM committee (known as the "House of the People"). The DSA would also "take over some of the administration work in the local authorities, municipalities, education and health departments, trade and business organizations, defence and judiciary systems etc". Composed of 22 representatives, each with a male and female deputy, the DSA sought to ensure "people from different backgrounds, nationalities, religions and genders [could] all participate" in an atmosphere of "peace, brother/sisterhood, satisfaction, and freedom".

The Social Contract approved by the DSA, meanwhile, asserted that "the areas of self-management democracy [did] not accept the concepts of state nationalism, military or religion or of centralized management and central rule". Instead, it insisted they were "open to forms [of political and social organisation] compatible with the traditions of democracy and pluralism, to be open to all social groups and cultural identities". In order to facilitate such a multi-cultural system of government, the contract also established: the separation of church and state; the prohibition of marriages under the age of 18; the recognition and protection of women's and children's rights; and the banning of female circumcision and polygamy. It also proclaimed that "revolution must take place from the bottom of society and be sustainable", and that equality, freedom, equal opportunity, and non-discrimination were the rights of all men and women. At the same time, all languages would be recognised, while prisons would be places of dignity,

rehabilitation, and reform. Furthermore, the rights of refugees would also be guaranteed.

[In the Cizîrê Canton, Baher explains, a "Greenbelt" policy had previously been imposed by the Ba'athist regime, in which the area would "only produce wheat and oils" (so its population could not diversify economically and challenge government domination). The "majority of people", then, were primarily "involved in agriculture in the small towns and villages", though some worked "as traders and shopkeepers in the bigger towns", and would have "very low" living standards. Meanwhile, Arab citizens had been brought in "from different areas to settle in Kurdish areas" from the 1960s onwards as part of an official Arabisation policy (which gave the newly-arrived Arabs permission "to confiscate Kurdish lands" and divide them between themselves).]

While there were problems with electricity in Rojava, because it had always been produced elsewhere under the control of the Syrian regime, citizens nonetheless had around "6 hours a day" worth of very cheap electricity (thanks to the TEV-DEM selling diesel at low prices "to anybody with a private generator on the condition they supply power to local residents at a very cheap rate"). Phone communication, meanwhile, was free, as "land lines [were] under the control of the TEV-DEM & DSA", and low-priced bread would be the main source of food.[51]

Having travelled to Qamişlo in Cizîrê Canton, meanwhile, Politis Daily foreign correspondent Evangelos Aretaios spoke in March 2015 about how the "**Rojava model [was] based on two main pillars**". The first, he says, was "**direct democracy as the basis of a communalist system in which citizens participate actively in decision-making** and the management

---

[51] http://libcom.org/news/experiment-west-kurdistan-syrian-kurdistan-has-proved-people-can-make-changes-zaher-baher-2

of the polis, from the neighborhood to the municipality and as far as the government". The second, meanwhile, was "**the denial of the nation state structure** and philosophy as such". And blossoming out of these principles was the commitment to giving "to minorities a participatory role unprecedented in the Middle East – a role as equals in the management of the polis".

Speaking to a 20-year-old YPJ fighter called Nupelda, Aretaios was told that women were effectively "fighting on two fronts": against Daesh and "against the conservatism and the sexism of the traditional Kurdish society that does not recognize the equality of the sexes". At the same time, twenty-two-year-old heavy weapons' platoon leader Heza asserted that she and her comrades were engaged in "**a war for freedom... not only for the Kurds but also for the Christians and Arabs and all the other communities living here in Rojava**". Additionally, she said, they were fighting "to have for all women equal rights with men in a society of equality and mutual respect". In short, they were struggling both "against the threat of pure annihilation" and "for a better society". In this way, Aretaios stresses, "**they are the only fighters in the region who are not fighting for the preservation and the continuation, in one way of another, of a status quo, but for a radical change**". In fact, he argues, it was perhaps "ideology [that was] the most effective weapon of the Syrian Kurdish fighters, women and men, against the barbaric indoctrination of Daesh".

Back in Qamişlo, Aretaios was accompanied by a budding journalist called Judy who asserted that "along with the fear, we have hope for… a future that will bring peace to all people living in Rojava". The young Rojavan also said that, while "we all help in one way or another…, **we are free to get organized in the Tev-Dem or not**". In other words, there was "no obligation" and "no social pressure to be part" of the progressive movement. "It's the first time we [have been given

73

an] experience [of] democracy", she stressed, and "**the first time across the region we women know what it is to have real, legal rights and to play a real role in public life**". [Such efforts had been made in the past, but not "from bottom to top", as "changes in women's status [had previously been] imposed by authoritarian reformers such as Ataturk, Shah Reza or the Baathists".] Although it would take years of improved education "to break the centuries-old traditions" of gender-related oppression and violence, she said, Rojavans had nonetheless "**entered for the first time on a forward path**".

In the People's Court of Qamişlo, meanwhile, "judge Ibrahim, his assistant and three lawyers" told Aretaios about how "**justice [was now working] much better than during the Assad regime**". Today, one of the lawyers said, "I feel like a real lawyer and not like the decorative accessory of a fake justice ceremony". For example, explains Aretaios, the new autonomous administration had "adopted a law that [had] expressly [forbidden] men to marry more than one woman", and another which had made "**women legally equal to men before the courts**". This development, he says, was "completely revolutionary" in a country in which "Islamic tradition" had previously been incorporated into law, making "the testimony of a man in front of a court... equal to the testimony of two women". In addition to "the legal and institutional changes", he stresses, "the widespread organization "Sara Against Violence" [had also] launched a huge fight to change attitudes in society and to stop physical and psychological violence and social pressures against women".

The humanitarian spirit of the Rojava Revolution, meanwhile, could be seen in the words of a preacher at a Syriac church in Qamişlo. When Jabhat al Nusra fighters had arrived in Serêkanîye two years before, he said, they had "proposed to the fighters of [the] YPG to leave them 24 hours in the Christian neighborhoods of Qamishli", insisting that they "would [then] withdraw without touching the Muslims". In their search to avoid a sectarian slaughter, however, "the YPG refused and continued the war", eventually liberating the city completely.

Another Christian, named Peter, would assert that "the government system of Rojava is the best for us Christians" and "for all peoples of Rojava, Kurds, Arabs, [and] Chechens" alike. "**It is a model for all of Syria**", he stressed, and one that "**could be a model for the entire Middle East**, which is emptying itself today of its last Christians". Maurice, meanwhile, insisted that, in Rojava, "**all [people] live together as brothers**". Speaking about how he participated in patrols in his neighbourhood "with [his] brothers the Kurds and the Arabs", he emphasised: "no one will separate us". One Kurd on patrol would then say that "**the groups of citizens to protect neighborhoods [were] composed of volunteers who [patrolled] all night**", stopping any cars entering the area that they did not recognise. Overall, though, Maurice added that there were "no dividing lines between Kurds and Christians and Arabs", with everyone helping each other, fighting for democracy, and hoping for a future "together".

According to Maria, the "**new administration [had given] Christians a status that [they had] never had**" in the past. They had "always lived on very good terms with the Kurds and Arabs", she asserted, but they had "never had such equality in administration and politics". The head of a Syriac Military Council (MFS) unit, meanwhile, who was "a veteran specialist sergeant of the Swiss army", stressed that, "in this war we are not just allies, we are brothers". The thirty-two-year-old fighter, called Johan, insisted that there were not "two different military forces working together", but parts of "the same body" that were fighting against barbarism together. "We believe in a better society", he said, and that had "already started with the building of the administration".

Abdulselam, meanwhile, who worked as a translator, affirmed that progressive Rojavans believed they could "change mentalities and traditions", and "make a difference in society". The fight against jihadists, therefore, was just "one aspect of Rojava", he said, and was all part of the "**effort to build... a third way between [Islamism] and secular authoritarianism**". And, although things would not change "from one day to another", he stressed, **the revolution had been "a radical break with the past"**, and had **"put down the first stones" in the struggle for "change and [a] democratic society"**.[52]

In December 2013, meanwhile, international human rights lawyer Margaret Owen had also travelled to Rojava. Two months later, she reported on her experiences, speaking about how 'internally displaced people' (IDP) from the Syrian Civil War had seen their lives ruined and been forced to migrate to Rojava. Many of the women she met there were widows, with husbands who had been "killed years before by the Turkish security forces" for being PKK members. In fact, she says, "many of the older widows" now had "children with the PKK in Northern Iraq", and claimed to be very "proud of [their] husbands, [their] sons and [their] daughters" who were fighting for their freedom and against the advances of jihadist reactionaries. There were also Arab families who had fled to Rojava, though, Owen affirms, and "several Arab villages on the border with Rojava [had even] joined the [PYD] and allied themselves with the YPG [in order] to oust al Qaida affiliates from their land".

[52] https://www.opendemocracy.net/arab-awakening/evangelos-aretaios/rojava-revolution#.VQbpYzPC9KE.twitter

Although it was "the only relatively safe region" in Syria, Owen asserts, "only a very few people, journalists or aid workers, [had] been able to visit" Syrian Kurdistan, with Turkey having "closed its border with Syria so the only entry point [was] through Northern Iraq" and "the semi-autonomous KRG [having] imposed restrictions on who could come and go" ever since 2012. Owen, however, had been "invited to spend a week in Rojava... by the co-chairs of the PYD..., Salih Muslim and Asiyah Abdullah". And, as an "advocate for women's, and especially widows', rights in conflict", she insists: "everything I learned about the PYD administration... impressed me". In particular, she praises the system of male and female co-chairs in "all associations, political, educational, medical, military, police, social and financial services". For her, this was "an excellent method of ensuring gender equality across the whole spectrum of society".

Owen also speaks of how, in each town and village, there was "a Women's House, where women and girls [could] access advice, counselling, protection, and shelter, in the face of many forms of gender based violence, honour killings, post-traumatic stress, and physical and mental health problems". She asserts that "domestic violence [was] widespread, especially among the IDPs, and many women [had] been victims of sexual violence". They had also experienced the "traumatic deaths of close relations, in prisons, on the battlefield, and through abductions and torture". Therefore, the significant support available for women in Rojava was a very positive development.

In addition to the "Women's Houses", she states, there were also groups called "Women's Academies", the "Families of the Martyrs", and "the Peace Mothers", which "all [worked] together to address this endemic violence and support the displaced without any outside humanitarian aid and on a completely voluntary basis". These associations, she stresses, had been "as crucial to the maintenance of Rojava's relative peace in the last few years as the armed fighters" of the YPG/YPJ. At the same time, she emphasises, Rojava was "**developing a progressive model for gender equality, religious and ethnic freedom, and participatory democracy unlike anything seen in the region**".

Unlike "the simplistic reforms suggested by some in the opposition" movement in Syria, Owen says, the Rojava Revolution had "the potential to secure far greater social justice". And this fact, she suggests, was probably the reason "why, perversely, it [had] so few international allies in spite of **massive popular support on the ground**". In short, she asserts, despite colonialist and nationalist attempts to "write the Kurds out of history and out of territory", the progressive process in Rojava was something that appeared to be here to stay.[53]

i) The Opposition in Rojava

Baher speaks about how sixteen political parties in Rojava had refused to join the DSA, and how they had "**total freedom to carry out their activities**", though they could not have fighters or militias (outside of the YPG/YPJ). The reason behind this stance was that, while Rojavans would generally be able to choose their own political path, there would be certain principles that were unnegotiable, such as **unity in the self-defence and security of the region**. The PYD and TEV-DEM both stressed, for example, that different groups "could [indeed] have their own fighters", but that they would have to be "under the control" of the YPG/YPJ (which were officially the defence forces of Rojava as a whole rather than just those of the PYD). The TEV-DEM, Baher explains, had taken this

[53] http://ceasefiremagazine.co.uk/gender-justice-emerging-nation-impressions-rojava-syrian-kurdistan/

stance because it **did not want competing militias to exist in Rojava**, especially considering that **such a situation had previously led to** "**many fights between different Kurdish organizations**" **in Iraqi Kurdistan towards the end of the twentieth century.**

Twelve of the parties mentioned above, Baher explains, had joined together and called themselves the "Patriotic Assembly of Kurdistan in Syria" (and were supportive of the bourgeois nationalist policies of KRG President and KDP leader Masoud Barzanî). In fact, Baher asserts, the KDP was still helping "some Kurdish people in West Kurdistan financially and with weapons training in an attempt to set up militias for some of the political parties in order to destabilize the area and its plans". In other words, the KDP-backed Kurdish nationalist movement in Syria could be seen (as asserted previously in this book) as a reactionary force trying to impede the progress of the directly democratic and socially-minded revolution underway in Rojava.

When Baher met with the majority of opposition parties, he asked them about the relationship they had with the PYD, DSA and TEV-DEM. **All of their responses**, he says, **were positive**. No arrests had been made, and there had been "no restrictions on freedom or organizing demonstrations". These opponents, however, told Baher that the PYD had cooperated with Assad's regime (a claim for which there was no evidence) and that it was a bureaucratic, authoritarian party (even though the PYD had "almost the same numbers and positions as any other party in the DSA"). Additionally, they claimed that the PYD had withdrawn from the KRG's 'Kurdish National Conference', which had been an attempt to unify all of the Kurdish forces in Rojava. The PYD and TEV-DEM refuted this assertion, though, insisting they had "evidence of a written document which [showed] that they [had] committed to the pact but that the opposition [had] not". In short, Baher asserts, **the nationalist opposition parties in question were simply stubbornly and dogmatically committed to the Iraqi KDP's stance**, and were unwilling to accept a more popular alternative in Rojava.

Other opposition parties, meanwhile, came from Christian communities, which had not joined the DSA or TEV-DEM but said "they [got] on well" with them and were "fine with their policies". They also affirmed their gratitude to the YPG/YPJ, who they said had "sacrificed their lives" to protect "everybody in the region" from both the Syrian army and Wahhabi terrorist groups like Daesh. At the same time, however, the Christian Youth Organisation in Qamişlo claimed that there was not "enough electrical power" and that youngsters did not have "much... to do or be involved in within the town". Nonetheless, Baher states, "the head of one of the political parties who was present in the meeting" asked the youngsters to remember they were "in the middle of a war", and that the most important thing was being able to "[sit] at home with no fear of being killed, [leave their] children on the streets, [and play] with no fear of being kidnapped or killed". In summary, this politician insisted: **"there is peace, there is freedom, and there is social justice"**, and all of the other citizens present agreed. Baher also spoke "to shopkeepers, businessmen, stall holders and people on the market", all of whom had a "positive view and opinion of the DSA and TEV-DEM", stressing they had **"peace, security and freedom"**, without **"interference from any parties or sides"**.

Meanwhile, Baher explains, the Iraqi government and the KRG had decided in 2013 to "dig a 35-kilometre long trench, over two meters deep and about two meters wide, on the Iraqi/Syrian border of Kurdistan", even though the YPG/YPJ forces had been valiantly protecting the area in question. The real reason for the trench, he suggests, was almost certainly to prevent PKK and PYD members from increasing their influence on the Iraqi side of the border and to "increase the effectiveness of the sanctions used against West Kurdistan in an attempt to strangle and pressurize them to the point of surrender".

KRG sanctions, Baher asserts, had effectively "crippled Kurdish life" in Cizîrê, leaving it without sufficient "medicine, money, doctors, nurses, teachers, technicians and expertise in industrial areas, especially in the oilfield and refining industry". At the same time, in spite of the canton's preparedness to sell wheat to Iraq at a very low rate, the Iraqi government remained committed to the blockade. In other words, the West and its allies in the region could not bear the thought of local people showing they could "rule themselves through direct democracy without [a] government and support from the US, Western countries and global financial institutions, like the IMF, WB and CBE (Central Bank of Europe)".[54]

ii) Parallel Structures in a Complex Regional Context

As Baher witnessed the effect that Rojava's progressive independence was having on society, Aretaios spoke to TEV-DEM member Cinak Sagli, who told him how the Rojava Revolution had aimed to **enable people "to participate actively in the various public services needed for the well being of community life"**. These services, he explained, ranged from collecting garbage to neighbourhood security and "from the distribution of heating petrol and electricity to women's rights and education". And, while "the communalist structure" of the TEV-DEM was "running parallel to and fully integrated into the government(s) and the parliament(s) of the three Cantons", Sagli asserted that there would be **no chance of any party exerting totalitarian domination in the region**

---

[54] http://libcom.org/news/experiment-west-kurdistan-syrian-kurdistan-has-proved-people-can-make-changes-zaher-baher-2

"if all the checks and balances... of the Rojava model... [were] successfully implemented".

At the "central administration" of the Cizîrê Canton in Amûdê, Aretaios saw the government building, which was "a cultural center transformed into offices, meeting rooms and [a] parliament". Here, he saw "a medley of Kurds, Arabs, Christians, Yezidis, even Chechens... in the rooms and the corridors of the Parliament and the government". With the system of "co-presidents or/and vice presidents", he stresses, there was an "**obligatory**" presence of women and "**representatives of different ethnicities or religions**" in the government. This principle, in turn, would make it "**very difficult for one ethnicity or religious group to overshadow the rest**", whilst "[guaranteeing] the role of women". In fact, in the "31st assembly of the Parliament, after the proclamation of the self-government in Rojava", Aretaios witnessed "three secretaries... **keeping the records of all the proceedings... in three languages: Kurdish, Arabic and Syriac**".

Although "the practical difficulties caused by the war" had meant the three Cantons of Rojava had to have separate governments at the moment, the general idea, "according to the majority of the people involved in the government", was to have, at some point, "**a (con)federate government for the three cantons**". Also written in the region's "Social Contract", meanwhile, was that the "democratic administration [did] not recognize the concept of the nation state". And, for Aretaios, "this **official renunciation of the nation state [was] one of the most important and deeply revolutionary dimensions of the Rojava experiment**".

Nonetheless, Aretaios explains, the Rojava Revolution also had "**a strategic vision of regional realities**", being ever aware that, "**if Kurds in Turkey and Syria insisted on a Kurdish independent state, they would immediately spark** hostile reactions from Ankara", Damascus, and most likely Tehran. At the same time, he says, such a demand would almost certainly "trigger reactions also from the international community". The fact that even the nationalist, pro-capitalist Kurds of Iraq had encountered so many difficulties in "persuading [not only] regional powers but also the US and the international community of their cause of independence", he stresses, "highlights the realistic limits of such efforts today in the region". Meanwhile, a search for Kurdish independence would suggest the desire to create a united Kurdistan, which would gloss over the fact that **the four different Kurdish entities had long "lived under very different regimes"**, experiencing "separate histories and trajectories". In particular, Aretaios asserts, "**the dominant socialist/radical ideology inspiring Kurdish politics in Turkey and Syria [was] very different [from] the dominant neo-liberal/traditional ideology of the Kurds in Iraq**".

"Getting organized in line with autonomy", Aretaios argues, was "**a form of realism** and of acceptance of complicated pan-Kurdish dimensions and the regional and international challenges". It was also realistic because the fact remained that **Kurds were "not alone"** in Rojava ("with Cizîrê Canton being the less homogenous of the three cantons" in the region, with 20% of citizens coming from ethnic minorities). Therefore, **a "classical" form of chauvinist and reactionary Kurdish nationalism (which "would try to create a nation state") would perhaps open the path to "acts of ethnic cleansing"**. In short, Aretaios claims, "**the nation state is not the prerequisite for democracy any more**", and the Rojava experiment is an acknowledgement of that fact. Furthermore, by stepping away from such 'nationalist' rhetoric, the cantons were "making a historical step in the region". The "biggest challenge of the people of Rojava", though, was the fact that they had been "**starting from square one and without any substantial help from [the] outside**" world (which was

83

refusing to acknowledge that "in the middle of a barbaric war something new [was] trying to thrive" – an attempt to "accommodate different needs and aspirations and to establish a multi-ethnic, multi-religious democracy").[55]

iii) Rojava's Communes and Councils

To ensure gender equality in Rojava, Baher asserts, the DSA, TEV-DEM, and PYD had all led by example, creating a system of "Joint Leaders" and "Joint Organizers" at "the head of any office". And, as a result of this **feminist philosophy, women were "heavily involved in every section of the House of the People, committees, groups and communes"**. In fact, Baher even says that women in Rojava had become the "most effective and important half of… society". In short, he emphasises, the belief system of the PYD (and the PKK) was that the **"equal participation of women in rebuilding society" was essential for bringing out "the best of human nature"**.

Rojava's communes, Baher says, were "**the most active cells in the House of the People**", and the TEV-DEM manifesto asserts that they are formed "on the principle of **direct participation** of [all] people". According to Baher, these bodies aim to develop and promote the different committees, and "search for solutions" regarding social, political, educational, and security matters, emanating from their own power and "not from the state". By organising themselves into "communes, cooperatives and associations", he says, they "create their own power". **All decisions**, meanwhile, **were made "openly" by all members of the community "older than 16 years old"**.

---

[55] https://www.opendemocracy.net/arab-awakening/evangelos-aretaios/rojava-revolution#.VQbpYzPC9KE.twitter

In Qamişlo, Baher speaks about how he had been to a commune meeting, where "there [had been] 16 to 17 people", of whom most were young women. They told him that their neighbourhood had ten communes, each consisting of 16 people, and that their job was to: meet people; attend weekly meetings; find out about problems; protect people and help to resolve their problems; collect rubbish; protect the environment; and attend "the biggest meeting to report back" about what had happened since the last meeting.

The commune members also insisted that they made "all the decisions collectively" and that no one intervened in that process. In one case, for example, they had wanted to create a small park, but the Mayor of the town could only offer them $100. As a result, they "collected another $100 from the local people", and many of them "collectively worked on it to finish it without needing more money". In another case, "the Mayor wanted to initiate a project", but the commune members told him they would have to "get opinions from everybody" before allowing it. Some people could not attend the meeting, though, so other commune members visited them to get their opinions. And in the end, the project was "unanimously rejected".[56]

At the end of January 2015, meanwhile, Janet Biehl spoke at New Compass about how her **Academic Delegation to Rojava** had met two representatives of the TEV-DEM in Qamişlo over a month before. Abdulkerim Omar and Çınar Salih, she explains, told the visitors about how progressive Rojavan activists "[understood] as Kurds that [their] problems [would] not be solved by creating a new nation-state", and that they were instead trying to "overcome [the] chaos [around them] with as little bloodshed as possible", and "**in spite of the existing state borders**". For that reason, they asserted that

[56] http://libcom.org/news/experiment-west-kurdistan-syrian-kurdistan-has-proved-people-can-make-changes-zaher-baher-2

they "prefer autonomy", and that "the solution has to be at the grassroots level".

According to Omar and Salih, "the nation-state system [had] created many prejudices, so people think Arabs and Kurds and Turks can't get along", and had reinforced the idea so that it became "wired into people's brains". Therefore, it was necessary to "create conditions for common life" and fight "to get rid of these prejudices", they said. Furthermore, they stressed, "a revolution that does not open the way for women's liberation is not a revolution". As a result of these beliefs, Rojavan activists had created a system that "rests on the communes, made up of neighborhoods of 300 people". In every commune, they explained, "there are five or six different committees".

Overall, Omar and Salih said, "communes work in two ways". Firstly, they sought to "resolve problems quickly and early—for example, a technical problem or a social one" that, if sent to a state, would usually "get caught in a bureaucracy". Secondly, they explained, decisions had to be "made at the bottom and then go up in degrees". And the communes aimed to be the closest thing to grassroots decision making, which would subsequently send their orders up to "district councils and city councils, [and then] up to the canton" level.

The city of Qamişlo, for example, had "6 different districts", and "each district [had] 18 communes" (which in turn were "made up of 300 people"). In other words, then, there were 108 communes in Qamişlo alone, serving (theoretically) 32,400 people. Each commune would have their own committees, like a health committee, and there would be "similar committees at higher levels" where the needs of each commune would be discussed. "That's how they make sure the canton administration's health committee has [a] direct connection with the needs of the commune", Omar and Salih stressed.

Each of these communes, meanwhile, had "2 elected co-presidents", who would then come together with other commune co-presidents "to make up the people's council of that district". Subsequently, the city's six councils would elect two of their own co-presidents, who would come together in the "citywide people's council of Qamişlo" (consisting of twelve people). In this city council, however, the plan was to have two hundred seats, so the remaining 188 would be filled by direct elections.

On the next level up, Omar and Salih explained, the 12 cities of Cizîrê Canton would come together for the "cantonwide people's council". The members of the city councils would elect two co-presidents, and then the other delegates for each city would be "allocated according to population". As Qamişlo was the biggest city, for example, it would get "more delegates than others", with twenty. In addition to the co-presidents of this city, then, eighteen more would be sent from Qamişlo to the canton-level council. "It's like a parliament", the two TEV-DEM members said, "but the ties between the commune and the councils are not severed". [At the time of the Delegation's visit, a census was still being done, and the cantonwide council did not yet exist.]

"Women's councils", meanwhile, existed "in parallel" to the people's councils "at all levels, the commune, the district, the city, and the canton". According to Omar and Salih, the councils would "discuss issues that [were] specifically about women". For example, in the case of "a social dispute, say about interpersonal conflicts", the regular committees would try to resolve issues immediately but, if the women's council at that level saw "in this committee an issue that [concerned] women, like a domestic violence dispute", they could step in. For instance, if they disagreed with the people's council, their authority would be respected in the final decision (even though the people's council itself had a 40% quota for female members). In other words, then, they had "veto power on issues concerning women". At the same time, if an issue could not be solved at a lower level, the issue would then go to court.[57]

Biehl speaks of her visit to Rojava ("as part of a delegation of academics from Austria, Germany, Norway, Turkey, the U.K., and the U.S.") as a journey to a "**society of social and political revolution**". Organised by activist Dilar Dirik and Devriş Çimen (head of Civaka Azad, the Kurdish Centre for Public Information in Germany), the trip saw the visitors take part in "an intensive tour of the various revolutionary institutions" in the Cizîrê Canton. In particular, Biehl describes the system of "popular self-government" based largely on "neighborhood commune assemblies…, which anyone may attend, and with power rising from the bottom up through elected deputies to the city and cantonal levels".

Having visited a "local people's council", the delegation noted how men and women "sat and participated together", with no gender division. They also "witnessed an assembly of women addressing problems particular to their gender", and realised very quickly "that the **Rojava Revolution [was] fundamentally a women's revolution**". The Yekitiya Star, for example, was "the umbrella organization for women's groups" in Rojava, and representatives for the organisation insisted that the "antagonist of women's freedom" was not patriarchy, but "the nation-state and capitalist modernity".

Later on, at a meeting of the YPJ, the visitors learned that "the fighters' education [consisted] not only of training in practical matters… but also in Democratic Autonomy". In other words, the militants were not only fighting to save their fellow citizens, but also to save their ideas. "Democratic Autonomy

[57] http://new-compass.net/articles/rojavas-communes-and-councils

in practice", meanwhile, Biehl insists, was **a practical ideology that seemed "to bend over backwards to include minorities, without imposing [itself] on others against their will,** leaving the door open to all". Although she concedes that the system in Rojava was not "above criticism", she asserts that, "as far as [she] could see, **Rojava at the very least [aspired] to model tolerance and pluralism** in a part of the world that [had] seen far too much fanaticism and repression". In short, she argues, "**to whatever extent it succeeds, it deserves commendation**".

According to Biehl, the economic model of Rojava was seeking to create a ""**community economy", building cooperatives in all sectors and educating the people in the idea**". At the moment, one adviser told the delegation, around "70 percent of Rojava's resources [had to] go to the war effort", but "the economy still [managed to] meet everyone's basic needs" nonetheless. One main reason for this achievement was the fact that, out of necessity (because of the regional embargoes on Rojava), **the cantons had been striving "for self-sufficiency"**. For example, the visitors went to see: "a sewing cooperative in Derik, making uniforms for the defense forces; a cooperative greenhouse, growing cucumbers and tomatoes; [and] a dairy cooperative in Rimelan". While the "abundant wheat supply" of Rojava "was cultivated" before the revolution, Biehl explains, it "could not be milled into flour" there because the Ba'athist government had built its mills elsewhere. Therefore, after the departure of regime forces in 2012, Rojavan progressives set about building a mill, "**improvised from local materials**", which now provided "flour for the bread consumed [in] Cizîrê, whose residents [got] three loaves a day".

At the same time, the Cizîrê canton had also been "Syria's major source of petroleum" before the Rojava Revolution, "with several thousand oil rigs, mostly in the Rimelan area". In yet another attempt to stifle local development in the region, however, "the Baath regime [had] ensured that Rojava had no refineries, [thus] forcing the oil to be transported to refineries elsewhere in Syria". In the last two years, though, Biehl says, "**Rojavans [had] improvised two new oil refineries, which [were] used mainly to provide diesel for the generators that [were used to] power the canton**".[58]

In November 2014, Alexander Kolokotronis spoke at New Politics about the political system in Hesîçe and elsewhere in the Cizîrê Canton. The city, he affirms, had a council "comprised of 101 people, as well as five representatives each from five other organizations including the PYD". There was also "a coordinating council", he stresses, "made up of 21 people". Hesîçe, meanwhile, had "16 district councils" consisting of 15-30 people, which would "meet every two months". At the same time, between 10-30 communes would "comprise a given district". In short, Kolokotronis notes, there was "**often 1 delegate for every 100 people in a district, which [was] far more direct than many other institutional structures across the world**".

The "most frequent" form of political activity, however, was "the convening of peoples' assemblies", according to Kolokotronis. This phenomenon, he says, which "also spans across Kurdistan" in areas influenced by the progressive Kurdish movement, served "as the base for Democratic Autonomy", and many areas had "**weekly peoples' assemblies**". And these structures, Kolokotronis reports, also send "delegates to the general council of Rojava", where "resolutions and decisions are preferred to be made by consensus instead of simple majoritarian vote".

In Hesîçe, meanwhile, "communes have commissions that address all social questions", from ecology and sanitation to

---

[58] http://kurdishquestion.com/kurdistan/west-kurdistan/my-impressions-of-rojava.html

"committees for women's economy to help women develop economic independence". According to the Alevi Academy for Belief and Culture's Aysel Dogan, Kolokotronis says, "the best way to create an ecological system is to build cooperatives". At the same time, "**other eco-minded activities include the development of seed banks, protesting the simple notion of nuclear power plan development, and the disallowing [of] the entrance of mining companies**" in the region. Furthermore, in an attempt to "foster an ecologically geared social consciousness", **education in ecological matters** "**is part of the explosion of academies and other learning institutions that inhabit the region**".

iv) Education and Economics in Rojava

According to Kolokotronis, "a number of academies [had] opened across Kurdistan", including "the Mesopotamian Social Sciences Academy in late August in Qamişlo", which sought to operate according to "an alternative education model". In the Cizîrê Canton alone, he asserts, "670 schools with 3,000 teachers" had begun "offering Kurdish language courses to 49,000 students" – something which had long been denied to Syrian Kurds. Meanwhile, "**youth councils, both under-18 and over-18, [had] emerged**", having a "say and power in the carrying out of initiatives and projects, e.g., in the building and modifying of recreational sites and spaces". In fact, Kolokotronis says, "some of the most radical perspectives have, with clear articulation and vision, come from the Kurdish youth", with one youngster stressing: "we don't consider ourselves nationalists. **We're socialist internationalists**". And indeed, while "Democratic Autonomy and Democratic Confederalism constitute an ideological and institutional push away from the State and capitalism", it is also a system based on solidarity, unity, and on a move "away from representative political structures to those of autonomous and performative practices".[59]

Reflecting on "the do-it-yourself nature of the revolution", and speaking of how it had been relying "on local ingenuity and the scarce materials at hand", Janet Biehl emphasises how education was a key part of this process. Having visited "the women's academy in Rimelan and the Mesopotamian Academy in Qamişlo", she and her colleagues had seen how schools were rejecting "ideas of hierarchy, power, and hegemony", with students teaching each other and learning "from each other's experience" (in a much more collaborative form of learning). Regarding "practical matters", though, Biehl says, "students learn what is useful" from their teachers while, with "intellectual matters", they are encouraged to "search for meaning". In short, rather than memorising information, "they learn to think for themselves and make decisions, to become the subjects of their own lives". In other words, Democratic Autonomy had sought to empower youngsters and turn them into protagonists in their communities.[60]

In December 2014, the Rojava Report republished an interview with Dr Amaad Yousef, the Minister of Economy for the Efrîn Canton of Rojava (who was "not a member of the PYD"). Kurdish communities had received very few opportunities prior to the Rojava Revolution, he says, but had not risen up against the Assad regime like some Arab citizens had asked them to because "the regime would [then] have said 'these ones want to break up Syria' and they would have organized all of the Arabs against us". Consequently, he notes, progressive Kurds said: "we are 15% of Syria and you are 85% of Syria. Let 50% of you rise up and [then] 100% of us will rise

[59] http://newpol.org/content/no-state-solution-institutionalizing-libertarian-socialism-kurdistan and https://armsforrojava.wordpress.com/2015/02/10/the-no-state-solution-institutionalizing-libertarian-socialism-in-kurdistan/
[60] http://kurdishquestion.com/kurdistan/west-kurdistan/my-impressions-of-rojava.html

up". As this did not happen, though, Kurds in Rojava played things very carefully, attempting to avoid an anti-Kurdish ethnic cleansing campaign. Therefore, they simply stated that they were "going to implement [their own] model on a democratic foundation and without bloodshed and that [their] door was open to those who wanted to join [them]".

In the first year of autonomy in Rojava, Yousef asserts, **progressive activists "founded a newspaper", a "TV channel", and "a people's assembly"**. At the same time, he says, they "threw out the regime elements among [them]", whilst doing no "harm to any place". As a result, "**secure and peaceful development** of commerce picked up pace" in Efrîn, with "**buildings [being] constructed and workshops [being] opened**". In fact, although only "450 thousand people [had been] living in Efrîn... before the revolution", the population soon "exceeded 1 million", with "close to 200 thousand Arabs" deciding to settle in the region.

Now, Yousef stresses, Efrîn had "50 soap factories, 20 olive oil factories, 250 olive processing plants, 70 factories making construction material, 400 textile workshops, 8 shoe factories, 5 factories producing nylon, 15 factories processing marble, 2 mills and 2 hotels". In fact, it actually became "**the first and only place producing soap in Syria**", he notes. The region was also "working on developing commerce around dairy products, fruit and other foodstuffs" in local villages, in the hope that refugees would return to their homes. At the same time, however, Yousef asserts that the administration had "[forbidden] the founding of any more olive factories from an environmental perspective", whilst also prohibiting "workshops melting lead [in order] to protect human health".

"**Engineers, agriculturalists and farmers**", meanwhile, had "**formed their own unions**", and, for the first time in Efrîn, **six trade unions "in the areas of health, commerce, agriculture,** sports and theater and music [had] been founded". Although "there was no other work outside of a couple of craft jobs" before the revolution, Yousef stresses, there was now "no unemployment [in Efrîn] with a population of over 1 million". In short, "everyone who wants can have a job", he says. In fact, he adds, Kurds who had previously gone to Damascus and Aleppo to find work (including "tailors, waiters, construction workers, doctors, [and] teachers") had now returned to Efrîn, even though "certain people [had] migrated to Europe".

"Interest", he asserts, was now "forbidden and no-one [could] charge it" legally. The local government, meanwhile, was "looking into the tax system from the Autonomous Basque Region", in which taxes would be "distributed to the ministries depending on the need". At the same time, there would be "transparency", so that citizens could "know where the taxes they pay are being spent".

Electricity generators, meanwhile, were "all over the canton and in every village", providing "at least 12 hours of electricity [per day]". At the same time, the local administration had "started a project to harness wind energy" and, "thanks to a popular cooperative that was founded together with the municipality, a dam [had been] built" to meet the water needs of the population. [Note that water had previously been "brought in with tankers".]

One example of the Efrîn administration's activity was when, during a jihadist siege, the price of a "sack of flour [had gone] from 3 thousand to 6 thousand 500 hundred (Syrian pounds)". As a result, he says, the canton management "immediately began working two mills and stopped the export of flour". Consequently, Yousef asserts, "the price of flour was brought back down to 3 thousand 500 hundred (Syrian pounds)". At the same time, while faced with high rents (as a result of migration to the canton), the autonomous administration had "begun preparations for construction cooperatives" and would seek to "ensure the right to housing for all".

Meanwhile, "a hospital belonging to the canton [had been] built", and "no fee [would be] taken from the poor in exchange for medical services", with "the fees taken from those who [had] the means completely [covering] the costs of the hospital". At the same time, "schools [had] been opened in all villages" and the autonomous administration also had "preparations to open a university".

Even though there were differences in pricing for those able to pay and those not able to pay, Yousef asserts, "everything produced in Efrîn is cheap". And, while "private capital [was] not forbidden", he says, it was "made to suit our ideas and system", which was being developed "around cooperatives and communes". They would "complete each other", he asserts. After the full development of the cooperative system, for example, "moral private capital [could then] be added in certain parts of the economy". In short, the government was seeking to progress slowly and pragmatically towards a fairer and more communal society, in an attempt to avoid more social upheaval.

According to Yousef, the gradual progress towards a more progressive society would help to ensure that more citizens would get on board with the project, and would eventually see Rojava "taken away from the liberal system". Such a system, he asserts, is one in which "the big fish swallows the small fish and there is no morality". For that reason, he stresses, "there is only one thing that is forbidden" in the Efrîn Canton, and that was "finance capital". Overall, he insists, it was important for Rojava's progressive activists to "build the system of a democratic nation", even though "a little time [would be] needed" for this process to occur.

95

Therefore, he emphasises, "**we will protect the rights of the poor and powerless and cooperatives and communities against the rich**", but "we cannot do everything in a day".[61]

[61] https://rojavareport.wordpress.com/2014/12/22/efrin-economy-minister-rojava-challenging-norms-of-class-gender-and-power/

6) Kobanî and Rojava's Fight against Daesh[62]

A global struggle, embodied in a city,
Humanity's hopes breaking through,
In a world of elites competing for power,
An alternative comes into view.

In early August 2014, Daesh launched an attack on the Yezîdî religious group in Şengal in north-western Iraq. This assault, in which "3-5,000 men [were] killed"[63] and "around 7,000 women and children were taken captive",[64] would see "40,000 Yezîdîs" leave Iraq for Europe in the following twelve months.[65] A "450,000-strong district", meanwhile, was soon "left with a population of just 10,000", with the majority fleeing further into the KRG or into Syria.[66]

To cut a long and horrific story short, the official army of the KRG (the Peshmerga) abandoned the Yezîdî population overnight when they heard about Daesh's advances on Şengal. "Family after family", for example, recounted "the same story of escape: While the Western media narrative [had] emphasized the US role and that of the Iraqi Kurds' Peshmerga fighters…, it was instead the [progressive] Kurds coming in from Syria and Turkey who saved the Yazidis' lives".

In other words, the "Kurdish coalition forces led by the PKK" were soon "being hailed as heroes" by the Yezîdî population, who proclaimed: "thank God for the PKK and YPG" and "the PKK saved us". Refugee Mikey Hassan, for example, spoke of how "the YPG had cleared a path through to Syria", while

---

[62] An in depth discussion of the YPG/YPJ's resistance in Kobanî and the complex political context surrounding it can be seen between Chapters 11 and 12 of *Rojava: An Alternative to Imperialism, Nationalism, and Islamism in the Middle East*

[63] http://www.dailymail.co.uk/news/article-2792552/full-horror-yazidis-didn-t-escape-mount-sinjar-confirms-5-000-men-executed-7-000-women-kept-sex-slaves.html

[64] http://jinha.com.tr/en/ALL-NEWS/content/view/27898

[65] http://rudaw.net/english/middleeast/iraq/040820151

[66] http://jinha.com.tr/en/ALL-NEWS/content/view/27898

other families insisted they had been "rescued from the mountaintop by YPG and PKK forces". Soon afterwards, Tracey Shelton reported at Global Post that the progressive Kurdish forces had rescued "at least 35,000 people".[67] In the words of Dilar Dirik, **the PKK and its Rojavan allies** had "**rescued an entire community** by displaying an alternative, more meaningful form of independence" than the nationalist KRG that had been supposed to protect it, "through **operating outside of the preset parameters of the state**".

For Dirik, the silence in the media about the Rojava Revolution and the PKK's resistance against Daesh elsewhere was "indicative of the fact that not much of this current concern [about Daesh] is based on genuine ethical commitments to human rights". In spite of the clear protagonism of the YPG/YPJ and PKK in rescuing the Yezîdîs, for example, the mainstream media and Western governments simply applauded unspecific "Kurdish fighters" for the mission, thus "lumping "the Kurds" into one monolithic category" and implying that the nationalists in the KRG (who were receiving all of the support from the West) were actually the ones who had been involved (when they had in fact been the ones who had left Yezîdîs to be massacred). Finally, Dirik says, "a mere bombing of the symptom [would] not get rid of the disease", and "the solution" for defeating Daesh had to "be radical and political and must include the recognition of actors such as the cantons in Rojava, as well as the PKK". Nonetheless, the PKK would still be labelled as a terrorist organization and Rojavans would still be blockaded, even though they had essentially "taught the international community a lesson in humanitarian intervention" and taught Kurdish nationalists "what real independence and autonomy [meant]".[68]

---

[67] http://www.globalpost.com/dispatch/news/regions/middle-east/140827/if-it-wasn-t-the-kurdish-fighters-we-would-have-died-there
[68] http://kurdistantribune.com/2014/islamic-state-sengal-how-pkk-ypg-taught-barzani-independence-really-means/

In fact, the rescue mission at Şengal would be far from the only PKK participation in Iraq's fight against Daesh. Even though the KRG was an ally of Turkey (which was an enemy of the PKK), the progressive group helped Peshmerga troops fight Daesh regardless. It would actually play "a vital role in guarding and regaining territory from the Islamic State".[69] One example would be in the small farming town of Makhmour, when the PKK came down from the Qandil Mountains in early August after a Daesh assault "to protect 12,000 Kurdish refugees from southeastern Anatolia, who [had] been living in a camp on the outskirts of Makhmour since 1994". In short, "the PKK [had] proven indispensable" in the fight against the Wahhabi jihadists.[70]

Perhaps in part due to the role of the progressive Kurdish movement in the fight against Daesh in both Iraq and Syria, the jihadists launched a vicious, heavily-armed attack on the northern Syrian town of Kobanî on September 15, 2014. Another reason, however, was almost certainly the fact that a "joint YPG-rebel command centre" had been established in early September between the Rojavan defence forces and progressive sections of the FSA, which would very probably have increased the "legitimacy of [the] YPG among local Arabs".[71] Finally, Daesh had already failed to take border towns from Rojavans elsewhere in Syria, and had decided to throw all it had at the YPG/YPJ in Kobanî.

i) The Important Role of the Media

The offensive soon resulted in "the fastest exodus" of the Syrian Civil War, with around a hundred and fifty thousand civilians fleeing for Turkey in the space of just one week.[72] The

---

[69] https://news.vice.com/article/meet-the-pkk-terrorists-battling-the-islamic-state-on-the-frontlines-of-iraq
[70] http://nationalinterest.org/feature/the-pkk-rumbles-northern-iraq-11169
[71] http://carldrott.wordpress.com and http://www.joshualandis.com/blog/whats-stake-kobani-islamic-state-kobani-calculations-carl-drott/
[72] http://widerimage.reuters.com/story/fleeing-islamic-state

Turkish State and international governments, however, continued to sit back and watch. The Daesh massacre of Yezîdîs back in August 2014, though, had attracted a significant amount of attention in the media (even though it was usually sensationalist and tended to omit the nature of the progressive Kurds' fight against Daesh). Kobanî, meanwhile, was in full view of the independent press across the border in Turkey, who gradually gave more and more coverage to the YPG/YPJ resistance in the city. And the more these progressive forces resisted the Wahhabi offensive, the more the media covered the story.

In short, the story of a fighting force actually being able to hold back the jihadists (after their lightning advances in Iraq and Syria in the previous few months) was becoming increasingly newsworthy for a Western press interested in sensational stories about anti-Daesh resistance. Of particular interest would be the role of the YPJ in the battle, which had seen women fighting alongside men on the frontlines, and showing immense bravery on numerous occasions. Dilar Dirik, for example, would soon speak of how Western tabloids were simply picking "the most "attractive" fighters for interviews", whilst 'exoticising' them as ""badass" Amazons" and paying "little attention" to their progressive politics. Essentially, she asserted, **the mainstream media was essentially "white-washing" and seeking to 'sanitise' the "radical struggle" of those defending the Rojava Revolution.**[73]

As a result of the increasing media coverage, the US government in particular was unable to repel claims from both sides of the political spectrum that it was allowing Daesh to cause a humanitarian crisis in Kobanî. Consequently,

[73] http://kurdishquestion.com/kurdistan/beyond-the-battlefield-the-kurdish-women-s-radical-struggle/380-beyond-the-battlefield-the-kurdish-women-s-radical-struggle.html, https://www.greenleft.org.au/node/57671, and http://www.aljazeera.com/indepth/opinion/2014/10/western-fascination-with-badas-2014102112410527736.html

Washington slowly began to respond, seeking primarily to ensure that the image of its leaders remained intact.

The leaders of the KRG, meanwhile, also realised that it was necessary to act. Having already repressed protests violently themselves since 2011, they knew that continued inaction and hostility towards Rojava while the largely Kurdish city of Kobanî was under siege could only bring more discontent in Iraqi Kurdistan. Facing the threat of Daesh expansion themselves, Kurdish Iraqis saw how their cousins in Kobanî were fighting back against the jihadists, and they made their voices of solidarity heard more and more as each day passed.

In Turkey, the government remained stubbornly against allowing Kurds, arms, or aid to cross into Kobanî. Protests, meanwhile, were becoming stronger and louder, and the state's repression harsher and more authoritarian. Clearly much more worried about the success of progressive Kurds in Rojava and the failure of Turkish-backed Islamists to overthrow Assad than the advances of Daesh, Ankara stopped journalists from entering into Rojava legally,[74] arrested refugees,[75] and even helped Daesh torture Rojavan civilians.[76] It also attacked journalists,[77] censured them,[78] arrested them,[79] and even killed them,[80] while murdering a number of protesters, cracking down on university activism,[81] and harassing and killing social activists.[82] And, finally, it "violated the ceasefire" with the PKK by launching airstrikes against it in early October.[83] Turkey's allies in NATO,

[74] http://topdocumentaryfilms.com/rojava-syrias-unknown-war/
[75] https://news.vice.com/article/turkey-arrests-274-kobane-refugees-fleeing-islamic-state-attack and @JM_Beck
[76] http://rojavareport.wordpress.com/2014/10/03/turkish-army-and-isis-working-together-torturing-civilians-around-kobane/
[77] http://www.bbc.com/news/world-middle-east-29499683
[78] http://kurdistantribune.com/2014/turkey-censors-twitter-websites-during-kobani-siege/ and @amybeam
[79] http://rojavareport.wordpress.com/2014/10/06/turkey-arresting-journalists-crossing-from-kobane/
[80] http://www.presstv.ir/detail/2014/10/19/382854/press-tv-reporter-in-turkey-killed/?utm_content=bufferb7e3f&utm_medium=social&utm_source=twitter.com&utm_campaign=buffer
[81] http://www.hurriyetdailynews.com/police-crack-down-on-kobane-protests-at-ankara-universities.aspx?pageID=238&nID=72743
[82] http://kurdishquestion.com/kurdistan/west-kurdistan/woman-killed-by-turkish-army-at-border.html
[83] http://www.theguardian.com/world/2014/oct/14/turkish-jets-bombard-kurdish-positions-pkk

however, pretended to ignore the state's increasing authoritarianism and the allegations of Turkish collaboration with Daesh.

From late 2012 onwards, insists Janet Biehl, the YPG/YPJ had been resisting jihadists in Serêkanîye (also on the border with Turkey), where a seemingly "Turkish operation" had seen Jabhat Al Nusra fighters enter the city "from the north" (i.e. from across the Turkish border). In other words, Rojava had become used to fighting back against Turkish-backed Wahhabi invaders over the course of its autonomous experiment, so Kobanî was nothing new for it. However, the big difference between Serêkanîye and Kobanî was that the former "scarcely registered in international media reports".[84] In short, then, **the question for the West and its regional allies was not now about saving civilian lives, but about stopping their reputations from running into even further disrepute.**

ii) The USA, Turkey, and the KRG Spring into Action

The first people to jump to solidarity with Rojava after the start of the Battle of Kobanî were PKK members or sympathisers (along with Turkish anarchists, socialists, and Marxists). Even a number of Western civilians would soon head to Rojava to volunteer with the YPG/YPJ. At the same time, moral and non-military support had come from the HDP, which had helped to organise events with intellectuals and trade unions to raise awareness about what was happening in Rojava. Feminists and LGBT activists also state their support for the YPG/YPJ's resistance in Kobanî and elsewhere.

---

[84] http://new-compass.net/articles/first-koban%C3%AA

Almost a month after the intensified Daesh assault on Kobanî had begun, the KRG said it had "dispatched weapons, equipment and humanitarian aid" to Kobanî,[85] while US forces had claimed to have hit Daesh targets near Kobanî as early as September 27.[86] Soon afterwards, on October 14, YPG spokesman Polat Can confirmed that the Rojavan defence forces were "officially working with the International Coalition against ISIS". Turkey, he insisted, had been the "serious obstacle" which had prevented "any help from reaching us" and had encouraged the USA not to launch air strikes in Kobanî.[87]

With some sections of the Left now claiming the YPG/YPJ were "collaborating with imperialism" by accepting US support, it soon became necessary to stress how, in the previous two years or so, these same voices had said nothing about the "cooperation, in both word and deed, between the United States, Turkey and the KDP around the Rojava question". As a result of the refusal of the PYD and its allies to submit to the will of these self-interested state powers, the Socialist Democratic Party's Rıdvan Turan insists, the people of Rojava were subjected to an "undeclared embargo". The silence of many left-wing voices about Rojava's "liberating and anti-imperialist stance", he asserts, was an example of "unredeemable social chauvinism". In short, they had ignored the Rojava Revolution when it had asserted its independence, but as soon as it accepted the temporary support of reactionary powers in order to avoid a massacre, they suddenly raised their voices.

For Turan, the US and KRG support accepted in Kobanî was not "collaboration" with imperialism, because it did not involve "entering into imperialist dependency and colonial

---

[85] http://www.ft.com/cms/s/0/51e16cc0-521c-11e4-b55e-00144feab7de.html#axzz3TvRtVbq3
[86] http://www.bbc.com/news/world-middle-east-29390781
[87] http://civiroglu.net/2014/10/14/ypg_usa/ and @mutludc

relations". It was merely a temporary convergence of interests (i.e. the fight against Daesh) which would only have an effect on the progressive experience of the Rojava Revolution if those pioneering it were to sell out their principles (which they did not seem prepared to do).[88]

On October 20, the USA made the decision to airdrop a limited amount of supplies to the Rojavan militias which had apparently been provided by "Kurdish authorities in Iraq"[89] (namely the PUK[90]). This act, which had been opposed by Ankara, showed how the superpower had become tired of Turkey's inaction (probably because of its awareness of the media damage it was doing), and soon pushed the AKP regime into adapting its strategy. Almost immediately after the airdrops, Ankara announced it was ""assisting" Iraqi Kurdish Peshmerga fighters to cross into Kobanî to join the fight" in Kobanî, supposedly as a response "to a request from the Kurdish president, Massoud Barzani".[91]

Days later, Peshmerga troops arrived in Kobanî, having passed through Turkey to reach Syria. Having been embarrassed by the PKK and YPG/YPJ back in August, the KRG was now looking to reassert the Peshmerga's previously perceived role as the fighting force most able to defend civilians in Kurdish communities. At the same time, the AKP was looking to deal with the negative press it had generated through its inaction and complicity with Daesh in previous months, whilst trying to prove to its NATO allies that it was prepared to make compromises.

Having held out for almost a month with limited arms and in spite of the Turkish embargo, the YPG/YPJ now had a chance to take back the parts of Kobanî lost to Daesh. Although they

[88] http://rojavareport.wordpress.com/2014/10/27/is-the-pyd-collaborating-with-imperialism/
[89] http://www.bbc.com/news/world-middle-east-29694594
[90] http://www.pukmedia.com/EN/EN_Direje.aspx?Jimare=22293
[91] http://www.bbc.com/news/world-middle-east-29694594

could have easily beaten the jihadists if supplies and reinforcements had been allowed to cross the Turkish border at the start of the siege, the air support from the USA and the ground support from the Peshmerga were nonetheless welcome as a solution (albeit imperfect) to Daesh occupation. By late January, the Wahhabi jihadists had been pushed out of Kobanî, and a deal had clearly been struck for the YPG/YPJ to continue receiving support from the skies during its expansion into other Kurdish communities previously taken by Daesh.

iii) Victories in Syria and Tensions in Turkey

On March 13, 2015, the Cizîrê Canton held its first municipal elections, showing that a certain level of stability had finally been established. Meanwhile, the YPG/YPJ continued to spread out from Kobanî towards the east, where it hoped to join the Kobanî Canton with Cizîrê. And, on **June 15**, the town of **Girê Spî** (Tel Abyad) was finally liberated from Daesh thanks to a "lightening advance" which connected the two eastern cantons of Rojava.[92]

The taking of Girê Spî came just one week after the **Turkish parliamentary elections**, in which the HDP finally crossed the electoral threshold and won 80 seats, "throwing a spanner in the works of Erdoğan's autocratic ambitions".[93] And the party had managed this achievement in spite of "some two hundred attacks on rallies, HDP campaigners, and party buildings" in the run up to the election, which culminated in "two bombs detonating in HDP offices in Adana and Mersin" and "two bombs going off at a huge rally in Amed/Diyarbakır" (which killed five people).[94] Towards the end of June, however, tensions rose even more between Turkey and progressive Kurds when **Daesh undertook "one of the worst massacres"**

---

[92] http://kurdistantribune.com/2015/gire-spi-liberated-from-daesh-kobani-celebrates-mourns/
[93] http://roarmag.org/2015/06/hdp-victory-turkey-elections
[94] https://www.jacobinmag.com/2015/09/erdogan-akp-hdp-isis-suruc-gezi/

of civilians in its history in Syria. The group's "suicide mission"[95] in Kobanî saw "around 30 jihadists" infiltrate into the city in disguise, setting off car bombs, waging gunfire attacks, and **"killing at least 206 civilians"** (**many of who were women, children, or elderly people**).[96]

Around two weeks later, the PKK stressed that the Turkish State had "dishonored the ceasefire… by building an excessive number of dams and security stations in Kurdish areas". Through a KCK statement, the group announced that "the Turkish government with its arbitrary actions [had] already resumed the war against the Kurdish people", and that it could "not remain silent" any longer.[97] The state's projects in the region, it asserted, were "aimed at displacing people and to help the Turkish military".[98] In short, the AKP's lack of commitment to actually taking steps forward with the 'resolution process' had now pushed the PKK to return to active military resistance against government occupation in Kurdish communities in Turkey.

Perhaps the tipping point for tensions in Turkey was the **Suruç Massacre** on **July 20**, when Daesh killed 34 activists brought together by the Federation of Socialist Youth Associations (SGDF), who were planning on travelling to Kobanî on a "five-day excursion" to "aid in the reconstruction of the city". Later, when "thousands of protesters rallied on Istanbul's Istiklal Avenue", Turkish police began "shooting tear gas, water cannon and plastic bullets at demonstrators".[99] KCK Executive Council Member Mustafa Karasu, meanwhile, said the "AKP was directly responsible because of its support to ISIS" over the previous months and years.[100]

[95] http://www.reuters.com/article/2015/06/26/us-mideast-crisis-syria-idUSKBN0P60UY20150626
[96] http://www.thedailybeast.com/articles/2015/06/28/isis-strikes-back.html
[97] http://rudaw.net/english/middleeast/turkey/120720151
[98] http://ekurd.net/pkk-says-turkey-violated-ceasefire-2015-07-12
[99] http://autonomies.org/en/2015/07/the-state-as-an-agent-of-murder-turkey/
[100] http://anfenglish.com/kurdistan/karasu-only-peoples-struggle-can-stop-the-dirty-wars-of-akp-and-isis

What followed was a state-driven escalation of tensions, with Ankara ordering the bombing of PKK positions in the Qandil Mountains of northern Iraq. PKK members had allegedly killed two policemen on July 23 as retaliation for the Suruç Massacre but, according to KCK spokesman Demhat Agit, these units were "local forces" which "organized themselves", were "independent from the PKK", and were "not affiliated" with the PKK.[101] Nonetheless, the right-wing Turkish media jumped on the wartime bandwagon, spreading fear and hatred for the PKK while Turkey's armed forces bombed both militant and civilian communities from July 24 onwards. In the town of Cizre, for example, the HDP reported 20 civilian deaths in just one week in early September,[102] while ABC News spoke about the "death and destruction" that the Turkish military had left behind.[103] Silopi was another Kurdish town where police had "opened fire indiscriminately on houses",[104] and Zergele had become the site of the murder of eight civilians on August 1.[105]

At the same time, the Turkish State had launched a crackdown on opposition forces, claiming that it was stepping up its fight against 'terrorism'. On July 30, however, the Associated Press affirmed that, "of the 1300 people detained…, only 137 were suspected of links to ISIS". The remainder, unsurprisingly, were "suspected leftists or Kurdish freedom movement activists".[106] At the end of August, meanwhile, the Human Rights Association (IHD) released a report which revealed that, "out of the 2,544 detainees" arrested by the State since July 21, only "136 [had been] accused of membership to ISIS", another 22 had been detained for belonging to the Gülen

[101] http://www.todayszaman.com/national_kck-official-says-pkk-not-responsible-for-murders-of-2-turkish-policemen_394957.html
[102] http://www.bbc.com/news/world-europe-34206924
[103] http://www.abc.net.au/news/2015-09-21/tensions-rise-in-kurdish-turkey-after-military-crackdown/6790752
[104] http://jinha.com.tr/en/components/3125655355/content/view/28147
[105] http://jinha.com.tr/en/ALL-NEWS/content/view/28254
[106] https://www.greenleft.org.au/node/59645

Movement, and "the rest [for associating with the] KCK/PKK and some other left-wing organisations".[107] In other words, **around 94% of those detained belonged to left-wing groups in Turkey.**

Then, just when the PKK was calling for a ceasefire at the start of October,[108] **two terrorist attacks in Ankara** killed at least 128 people who were marching "against war and AKP's hostile and violent policies", in a protest "organized by democratic NGOs including KESK, DISK, TMMOB and TTB" which the HDP "had strongly supported". Just after the march had begun, "two bomb attacks occurred among HDP cortege", creating suspicions that "the main target of the attacks" had been the HDP. According to the progressive party, the "AKP's policy of relying on radical groups [i.e. "ISIS, Al-Nusra, and Ahrar Al-Sham"] as proxies" was "at the heart of today's tragedy".[109] Meanwhile, the KCK declared, in spite of the bombing, "inaction on condition that no attacks are carried out against the Kurdish movement, people and guerrilla forces".[110]

In short, the tensions in Turkey were now spiralling out of control, being fuelled by both nationalist and Islamist hatred for the secular and progressive movements of the HDP in Turkey and the Rojava Revolution in northern Syria. In particular, Kobanî had been a turning point in the AKP's time in power, revealing to Kurds once and for all that the Islamist party was not at all interested in resolving the Kurdish Question in a peaceful, democratic manner. Instead, Kurdish communities had seen the AKP (and the Turkish State) for what it was: a repressive, power-hungry, and authoritarian organisation, determined only to consolidate its own power.

---

[107] http://www.kurdishinfo.com/ihd-releases-balance-sheet-of-war-in-turkey-for-one-month
[108] https://uk.news.yahoo.com/pkk-leader-says-ready-turkey-ceasefire-123742433.html#X0vZQT7
[109] https://hdpenglish.wordpress.com/2015/10/12/call-to-the-international-community/
[110] http://anfenglish.com/kurdistan/kck-declares-inaction-on-condition-of-not-being-attacked

7) Why Should We Defend Rojava and the PKK?[111]

The power of the People, autonomy, choice,
Cooperation and dialogue key,
The past is the past, let's discuss where we're at,
As we are what we're striving to be.

In the previous chapters, I have shown that the Rojava Revolution, for all its imperfections, is an inspirational democratic experience. I have also suggested that the PKK has become perhaps the most progressive mass movement in the Muslim World. Nonetheless, I would not expect the reader to support these assertions without first looking at the criticisms of both the Rojava Revolution and the PKK.

Zaher Baher, for example, offers up some popular criticisms, whilst remaining broadly sympathetic to the progressive experience in Rojava. The TEV-DEM, he explains, was responsible for setting up both the communes and the DSA, and saw the latter "as the executive body" which would simply implement the decisions made by TEV-DEM organs (rather than making top-down rulings). However, while the PYD and PKK (both disciplined forces thanks to years of underground resistance) had been the driving forces behind the 'bottom-up' TEV-DEM, Baher raises doubts about the hierarchical structures still within those organisations, in which the leaders largely determined the actions of the rank and file.

Some anarchist dogmatists argued that the PKK would have to dismantle its own party structure and become a decentralised federation of local organisations before they could lend it support. The **TEV-DEM** in Rojava, however, which was

---

[111] An in depth discussion of the characteristics of the PKK and the Rojava Revolution can be seen in Chapters 9 and 10 of *Rojava: An Alternative to Imperialism, Nationalism, and Islamism in the Middle East*

essentially a PKK-inspired organisation, included many people who had "not been members of the PKK or PYD". Furthermore, it was essentially **all about consultation, with its members making all of the decisions** before then telling the DSA what to do.[112] In short, it was far from hierarchical.

To clarify the doubts outlined above, Brazilian professor Bruno Lima Rocha spoke in February 2015 about the under-discussed "anarchist party model", which was aimed at promoting both "self-management and direct democracy". In spite of the apparently hierarchical structures of the PKK, he asserts, "**nobody should understand [it] as a kind of "good intentions only party""**. Instead, he argues, it (and the TEV-DEM in Rojava) should be considered as "a strategic conception guaranteeing that party cadres and **structures will be put in [the] service**" of the People, with the duty of helping to build more effectively a set of "new political institutions based on a horizontal and egalitarian society". Such a model, he notes, could be named "organicism, platformism, [or] specifism", and saw party units undertake the responsibility of "**[reinforcing] the mass struggle which must be taken up by the whole communities**, allowing people to lead their own destiny by and through the people's assemblies". The closeness of the 'anarchist party model' and the structures of the PKK, Rocha asserts, "can be easily detected in a simple reading of documents from both the PKK and anarchist traditions".[113]

Baher, meanwhile, also raises doubts about Öcalan's role as an almost spiritual leader of the progressive Kurdish movement, but emphasises that the imprisoned ideologue himself had said: "everything can be criticized and rejected". The Rojava Revolution, Baher insists, "was not [only] Öcalan's idea", and

[112] http://libcom.org/news/experiment-west-kurdistan-syrian-kurdistan-has-proved-people-can-make-changes-zaher-baher-2
[113] http://kurdishquestion.com/index.php/kurdistan/bridges-between-anarchism-and-democratic-confederalism.html

had been consciously taken on as a project by the people. Thus, while citizens respected and even revered Öcalan, they would prevent an elite-driven corruption of the revolution if they followed the Democratic Confederalist principle of taking control of their own lives and not allowing others to make decisions for them. And if the teachings of the PKK leader had inspired people to think and act in such a way, it is difficult to consider Öcalan as a counterrevolutionary figure. Of course, if Öcalan were hypothetically to leave prison and seek to dominate the progressive political experience in Rojava (or elsewhere) according to his own whims, such actions should obviously be opposed by activists on the Libertarian Left. This concept is pure imagination, however, and is very unlikely to happen in reality (and is therefore fairly irrelevant to the discussion).[114]

Janet Biehl, meanwhile, also stressed that it had made her feel uncomfortable to see images of Abdullah Öcalan so often in Rojava. Nonetheless, she insists, "to interpret those images" as indoctrination would be "to miss the situation entirely". Öcalan, for example, had insisted himself that "no one will give you your rights", and Rojavans she had spoken to were therefore aware of the need to "educate both themselves and society". In other words, by following the "set of principles" which Öcalan had taught them, they were now working out "how to implement it" and empowering themselves in the process.

In a context of "torture, exile, and war" under nationalist regimes in the region, Biehl insists, Öcalan had simply "taught [people] how to reset the terms of their existence in a way that [would give] them dignity and self-respect". And it was primarily for that reason that many citizens throughout Kurdistan held him in such high regard. That did not mean

[114] http://libcom.org/news/experiment-west-kurdistan-syrian-kurdistan-has-proved-people-can-make-changes-zaher-baher-2

they were not independently minded, however, and Biehl herself insists that the Rojavans she and her delegation had met were more than "accustomed to grappling with hard questions". In fact, in her opinion they consistently **responded "thoughtfully" and even welcomed critique, showing a great amount of open-mindedness and intellectual independence.** The system they were establishing, meanwhile, was "an endeavor that [was pushing] the human prospect forward" and "setting a new standard for what human beings [were] capable of" achieving. In short, she says, the Rojava Revolution was shining "as a beacon… in a world fast losing hope".[115]

Aware of the challenges facing the revolution, meanwhile, Baher insists that habits cultivated in capitalist societies would take time to fade away, and there would be no immediate solution to that issue. However, to facilitate the success of the most progressive elements of the Revolution, he believed "**the communes must increase their roles, duties and powers**". Once they had control of crucial resources like wheat and oil, he stresses, they could become a safeguard against self-interested elites in society, ensuring that enough food and energy was distributed to everyone in the community. Only after this point, he asserts, would they be able to "sell it, exchange it for necessary materials for the people or just simply store it for later when needed".

In present-day Rojava, though, Baher stresses, **people were experiencing peace, freedom, and cultural change, and the Revolution was thoroughly underway.** People there were adapting to: "a culture of living together in peace and freedom"; "a culture of tolerance and give not just take"; "a culture of being very confident and defiant"; "a culture of belief in working voluntarily and for the benefit of the

---

[115] http://kurdishquestion.com/kurdistan/west-kurdistan/my-impressions-of-rojava.html

community"; "a culture of solidarity and living for each other"; "and a culture of, you are first and I am second" (so that people are driven more by the common good than by selfish goals). Although life was difficult thanks to the war and the embargoes, "the gap between rich and poor [was] small", and people were generally upbeat and happy. And, perhaps most importantly, they had now experienced a system in which they were being encouraged to make decisions for themselves, and would thus "resist the return of the culture they used to live with before".[116]

i) Understanding Reality and Giving Critical Solidarity

For author Showan Khurshid, Syria and the wider Middle Eastern region effectively had to choose between three realistic options on the ground: Rojava's secular and democratic model; a continuation of the pre-Arab-Spring status quo of nationalist or Western-backed dictatorships; or the rule of Islamists (and probably violently discriminatory Wahhabi ones, at that). If the battle for human rights (with an emphasis on women's rights) in Rojava were lost, therefore, "the freedom loving world [would also] lose a lot", he asserts.[117]

This focus on 'facts on the ground' was not always popular with some left-wing ideologues, who argued that progressive Kurds in Syria, Turkey, or elsewhere should actively resist all forces of oppression, rather than trying to build autonomous structures in spite of these regional powers. However, just a quick analysis would leave us with the reality that, faced with the intense hostility of the Turkish State, for example, failing to seek a military détente with Ankara would effectively impede the PKK's project from taking root on the ground – and send Kurdish communities once again into a horrific, futile, and

---

[116] http://libcom.org/news/experiment-west-kurdistan-syrian-kurdistan-has-proved-people-can-make-changes-zaher-baher-2
[117] http://ceasefiremagazine.co.uk/gender-justice-emerging-nation-impressions-rojava-syrian-kurdistan/

unwinnable contest with NATO's second largest army. In short, favouring peaceful negotiation and a parallel construction of an alternative from the ground was (while unpopular with more dogmatic left-wingers) a sensible, pragmatic decision.

To suggest solidarity with the masses and not with the progressive Kurdish movement linked to the PKK, meanwhile, would be to ignore the fact that the former had organised and acted precisely because of the encouragement of the latter. While left-wingers can and should criticise certain elements of the PKK's past (and even present), then, to overlook or even deny the role that the group has played in proposing and implementing an alternative model for the region would be completely irrational. The simple fact is that the PKK and its allies are the biggest progressive mass movement on the ground in the Middle East, and there is no alternative on the same scale. Therefore, to collaborate with only those forces which had absolutely no links with the progressive Kurdish movement would be to collaborate with only a handful of people without a central role in the revolutionary process in Rojava.

Along these lines of understanding, the Anarkismo.net Editors Group (AEG) outlined in November 2014 why the Rojava Revolution was "a very important and inspiring struggle". As a result of the PKK's transformed ideology, the AEG insists, "the large platformist and especifista network around Anarkismo.net" had decided to support the progressive Kurdish movement, "although not uncritically", in spite of the fact that it was "not explicitly, or even thoroughly, anarchist". The group then defends its stance by asserting that its members "support struggles against oppression in principle", even if the oppressed were "to choose approaches we might not agree with". In short, it stresses, the oppressed and the oppressors can and should never be seen as equal evils, even when the former adopt incredibly reactionary measures. The fact is, it argues, that **"all struggles are internally contested and imperfect"**, as "the oppressed are not politically or socially homogenous". **Solidarity**, therefore, **"is about comradely assistance"**, **not about "closing dialogue or excusing errors"**.

Essentially, the AEG argues that **"there is a sliding scale" of the acceptability of currents struggling against oppression**, and that some of these will logically receive more support from its members than others. In other words, the group stresses, **"the closer an organised current is to our positions, the more we support them and show solidarity"**. At the same time, though, "there are some political positions that are simply unacceptable", and AEG members would establish no relations with groups proposing such stances.

The AEG's own belief in a particular political programme, it emphasises, would not mean refusing solidarity to progressive forces that did not share such a view. In spite of "its limitations", the group insists, the PKK and its allies were "far from a top-down authoritarian regime in the making" and were, in the end, "fighting on the right side". Essentially, it stresses, the "issue is not whether the PKK is 100% anarchist", because "it is certainly not", even though there are definitely "elements of the PKK programme that anarchists [could] gladly support". The real issue, it asserts, is that a 'purist position' ignores the reality that **"politics is a messy situation, based on debate, conflict and compromise"**, and that the wait for a perfect movement or moment to arrive would be an incredibly long one. Instead, it says, libertarian socialists must try to "navigate", whilst maintaining their own principles, "a more complicated reality, marked by partial gains and messy struggles".

ii) Resisting Dogmatic Critiques

Negative arguments from some on the left (i.e. that the PKK and its allies were "authoritarian", "patriarchal", or "ethno-nationalist") did not often "derive from a balanced engagement with the evidence". One claim, for example, had come from a "Turkish ultra-nationalist website hostile to the PKK – and a book attacking Öcalan" (whose author provided "no evidence except what he admits are "rumours" without confirmation"). At the same time, the AEG argues, the PKK had "never really fitted" a mould of "ethno-nationalism". The very multi-ethnic nature of the TEV-DEM, meanwhile, was simply one piece of evidence to discredit such claims. Furthermore, while men had a "prominent role... in leadership positions" in the PKK, the AEG stresses that "**there is more to a movement's position on women's liberation than a head count**". In short, while the PKK and its allies operate "in a context in which the subordination of women is actively promoted by many forces – not least the Islamic State/ISIS – **the PKK has** nonetheless **actively promoted equality for women in its armed forces, structure and ideology**".

In short, "**to the extent that any force is fighting for women's liberation in Rojava, it is the PKK**". The progressive Kurdish movement, the AEG asserts, "**pioneered the movement for women's liberation in Kurdistan**". In other words, "**those areas where the PKK does not have a major presence are very patriarchal**, whereas those where the PKK has a presence are not".

Regarding the PKK's past, the AEG says, the fact that the party had certain origins or influences does not mean "that is currently the case". As an example to support this point, the AEG refers to how groups can change, with the Zapatistas in Mexico originally having come "from a Maoist approach",

116

while "Mikhail Bakunin himself was originally a Slavic nationalist". Therefore, the group asserts, "**the past is not always a good guide to the present, especially when other aspects of the past are ignored**". It also stresses that "people and organisations change politically and it is [sometimes] irrelevant what they were". If we look at the PKK's past as a guide to what it is now, the AEG adds, we must also examine its transformation in the early twenty-first century, and the fact that the party has significantly "critiqued its past" and been "**brutally honest about [its] own past flaws**". Such analysis, the AEG emphasises, "is very promising and shows **political maturity**". In other words, "while the PKK were not perfect, and still are not, they have reflected and changed" and, essentially, only "**what they say now and what they do now**" truly matter.

If libertarian socialists always engaged situations and movements according to how they "would like them to be", the AEG says, they would never "deal with the complex realities" behind such movements and circumstances, and never "grapple with this reality" in an effective way. The simple fact is, it maintains, that "**most major movements today**" are not exactly how many on the libertarian left would want them to be. Therefore, if such progressives followed the type of dogmatic approach outlined above, they would almost always "isolate themselves, and do so proudly", whilst cutting themselves off from potential comrades.

The AEG gives the example of apartheid South Africa to support its argument, emphasising that, "whatever the limitations of the forces that led the anti-apartheid struggle…, they were progressive compared to the apartheid regime". In short, they were "fighting against a monstrously oppressive system", and were thus "infinitely preferable to that system". Neutrality under such circumstances, therefore, would have been to act "as if there was no difference at all between oppositional popular forces, like trade unions and community movements, and the apartheid regime". Just as such indifference would have represented a "serious loss of perspective" back then, the AEG asserts, it represents a serious loss of perspective today with regards to Rojava, as the PKK has, "in all of its incarnations…, fought against the severe national oppression of the Kurds in Iraq, Iran, Syria and Turkey" from the very beginning.

Of course, the AEG insists, libertarian socialists should never become "cheerleaders and blind supporters" or stop making their own independent critiques. In showing solidarity with the PKK and the project of its allies in the Rojava Revolution, then, "critical engagement" must occur whilst a libertarian socialist stance is made clear. In short, **progressive activists must stand alongside "the PKK and the Rojava Revolution against the forces of the Islamic State/ISIS, of Turkey, and of Western imperialism"**, whilst not becoming an uncritical "PKK auxiliary".

In other words, the AEG supports a realistic analysis of the current situation on the ground, insisting that the "**best outcome in the real world Rojava would be the victory of democratic confederalism**, opening up space for further changes, and inspiring rebels elsewhere". However, other options would still be a step forward from the Assad regime. The "second best" possibility, for example, "would be a PYD-led state", while "the third best would be a victory of the Kurdistan Regional Government (KRG)". Both of these, the AEG asserts, would be better than Western and Turkish-backed Islamist rebels from taking control and, "at the worst end of the spectrum would be the victory of the Syrian dictator, Assad" or "the victory of the Islamic State/ISIS". The possibilities outlined above, meanwhile, are **the only truly possible outcomes of the conflict.**

In the real world context, then, where the creation of a utopian society "is a very distant prospect at best", the AEG insists, **the libertarian socialist movement "will have to be forged and shaped in the reality of struggle, and may differ in some ways from the ideal vision"**. In short, the group stresses, any viewpoint on the Left which does not grapple with actually existent movements is one "divorced from reality". Therefore, libertarian socialists "need to **meet [the working class] where it is** if our ideas and practices are to have any relevance".[118]

LSE professor David Graeber share this view, insisting that, "if there is a parallel today to Franco's superficially devout, murderous Falangists", it would be Daesh, and "if there is a parallel to the Mujeres Libres of Spain" during the Spanish Civil War, it would be "the courageous women defending the barricades" in the cities and towns of Rojava. And for him, as with the AEG, the international left must not be "complicit in letting history repeat itself".[119]

Whilst seeking to maintain as objective an analysis of the PKK and its role in the Middle East as possible, I have sought to echo the points made immediately above. The PKK and its allies, for instance, are indeed imperfect, but they are without a doubt on the 'right side of the battle' – fighting against oppression, exploitation, and ethnic and religious discrimination. In fact, they are the most progressive mass movement active in the Muslim World today. Of course, we will only see the full effect that adapting to changing circumstances and realities on the ground has played in the development of the revolutionary process in Rojava in the coming months and years. However, it is certain that, without international solidarity from the Left, the Rojava Revolution's chances of survival will be much lower.

---

[118] http://anarkismo.net/article/27540
[119] http://www.theguardian.com/commentisfree/2014/oct/08/why-world-ignoring-revolutionary-kurds-syria-isis

Conclusion

In this book, I have sought to present in straightforward language the main causes of injustice in the Middle East, and provide the reader with a general outline through which to understand the context better. I have also aimed to show how the Rojava Revolution has presented the region with a unique and innovative way of breaking free from the current environment of oppression and violence.

Overall, it is important to point out that the revolution in Rojava is not perfect, and that the inspirational ideas it holds so dearly have not yet been (and may not be) entirely implemented. In fact, there are a large number of obstacles that the process has faced already, and that it is likely to continue facing in the future. As Rojavans move forward, they will need to confront: the persistence of nationalism, feudalism, and chauvinist conservatism in some sectors of Kurdish society; the seemingly excessive veneration of Abdullah Öcalan in pro-PKK circles; the pseudo-religious bigotry spread in neighbouring areas by Daesh and other right-wing Islamist reactionaries; the erroneous belief among some citizens in the benevolent intentions of Western political elites in the region; and an incomplete (or absent) understanding among some sectors of society of the fundamentally anti-democratic nature of the capitalist system.

At the same time, the progressive and directly democratic elements of the revolutionary process must eventually, in times of reduced conflict, ensure an end to military conscription (put in place primarily due to wartime desperation and necessity) and a reduction in (or elimination of) the power of state-like institutions created in autonomous Rojava. And, finally, the Revolution will have to prepare for the possible continuation of a centralised Syrian State (whether under Ba'athist, Islamist, or nationalist control), whilst resisting and challenging the self-interested schemes of international and regional powers to ensure their own economic (and political) concerns and activities in the Middle East are protected.

With so many obstacles ahead of them, therefore, it may indeed seem like Rojavans (in the process of creating progressive, secular, and directly democratic structures) have all the odds in the world stacked against them. Nonetheless, international sympathisers must remember that the region has already survived a long and painful economic embargo imposed upon it by Turkey and the KRG (largely supported by their Western allies). Furthermore, we must also acknowledge that Rojava's isolated, under-armed, and underfunded defence forces managed to hold Daesh (and other Wahhabi jihadists) back almost entirely on their own for years until US-led airstrikes increasingly pushed the group out of Iraq (and into Syria) in late 2014. In fact, in spite of the extreme hardships they had already faced, the YPG/YPJ resisted Daesh alone in Kobanî for weeks (completely surrounded and cut off from the support they could have received from their allies elsewhere) where much better-financed and better-armed forces elsewhere in the region had resisted the jihadist group for hours or days. In short, we must not forget, and we must certainly not underestimate, the spirit and determination of humans to persevere through adversity when they have dreams of progress in their hearts and minds.

Using Our Dignified Rage

As I have carefully considered the situation in the Middle East while writing this book, the people of Rojava have helped to strengthen my belief in humanity and my hope for a better world. In fact, their courage and compassion amidst the death and destruction so commonplace in my research has even brought me close to tears on a number of occasions. Whether it was the fighter sacrificing his life for his comrades by dropping a grenade into an Daesh tank; the women fighting to their last breath when surrounded by jihadi militants; or the middle-aged couple saying their bodies may have been in Turkey but their hearts were with their twenty-year-old daughter fighting with the YPJ in Kobanî, **the stories of heroism are both abundant and inspirational**. Furthermore, the unity that has been forged in Rojava between Kurds, Assyrians, Arabs, Turkmen, and others has been truly inspirational.

At the same time, the fact that so many of these unified, autonomous forces have been slaughtered barbarically by the brainwashed and bigoted fighters of Daesh merely increases in my heart what the Zapatistas have called **'dignified rage'**. Consequently, this feeling (which is a response to the horrors we experience in life and can only be useful if it inspires in us a will to fight with all our hearts for justice, unity, equality, and freedom) has served to convince me that there is no other way in which I would prefer to spend my time than in the service of truth, progress, and revolutionary solidarity.

Overall, it is very clear that the survival of the autonomous, democratic, and libertarian socialist experience in Rojava depends on how the Syrian Civil War and the Daesh insurgency develop in the coming months. Whether the progressive political experiment survives or not, however, the fact is that it has given people in the Middle East and throughout the world a **concrete example of the path the region (and the world) must follow if it is to attain justice and peace**. The only way in which working people can truly escape oppression and exploitation is if they **govern themselves and have control of their own land and their own resources**. And they can only govern themselves in peace if they **cooperate with each other, and encourage unity between all individuals – regardless of their ethnicities,** traditions, or religions. In short, only by unifying around principles of justice and equality for all will individuals be able to resist the power of imperialist nations, fight back against exploitative regional elites, and extinguish the threat of religious or ethnic sectarianism.

If we truly wish to support the revolutionary experience in Rojava, therefore, we must avoid falling into the trap of supporting Western political elites with their continued interference in the Middle East. We must also avoid praising or pardoning existent regimes in the region which have committed their own crimes. Most importantly of all, however, **we must spread the word about the progress Rojavan communities have made**, and we must encourage international solidarity towards their inclusive revolution and their resistance to the brutal, authoritarian forces of Daesh.

The Purpose of This Book

The only thing I ask of you, the reader, is to reflect on the words of this book and come to your own independent conclusions. At the same time, though, I hope you will support humanity's search for peace by embracing equality, justice, and people's democracy, whilst opposing discrimination, exploitation, and authoritarianism in all their forms. And one of the best ways to do that today is to be aware of movements pursuing that same goal, to share knowledge about them with those around you, and to do whatever you can to support them – whether in your local community, within your own country's political structures, or through direct contact.

Fear and ignorance will always be exploited, both by the world's dominant economic and political elites and by reactionary chauvinists. The best way to combat these forces, then, is to fight against both fear and ignorance, by spreading both hope and truth whilst exposing and criticising all oppression, injustice, and exploitation in the world – realities that will always strengthen imperialists and reactionaries (whether pseudo-religious, political, or ethnic). As long as there is ignorance, for example, the fear felt by the world's citizens will continue to be misdirected (often with the help of mainstream media misinformation or manipulation) towards supporting further government control over their lives and continued interference (in the case of imperialist nations) in the politics of other countries. Therefore, I have written this book with the aim of spreading truth and supporting the informed resistance of the reader to a human consciousness too often based on lies.

At the same time, though, I am not a dogmatic or disconnected optimist. It is the never-ending search for reason and evidence that has led me to support what I support and oppose what I oppose. In the words of historian Tim Stanley, "power corrupts everyone: Left, Right, men, women, gay, straight, black, white, religious, atheist".[120] And that fact, backed up by a knowledge and understanding of the past, has definitively made me an advocate of freedom and popular democracy. Simply speaking, when power belongs to everyone and no-one simultaneously, there is no possibility of it being abused in the way it has been under authoritarian political leaders throughout human history. However, destroying elite domination also requires us to encourage enthusiastically the values of solidarity, equality, and cooperation to take root.

The main reason for my continued hope in a progressive model for humanity is that, as Uruguayan writer Eduardo Galeano has said, utopia is like the horizon.[121] In other words, although we walk towards it without ever truly reaching it,

---

[120] http://blogs.telegraph.co.uk/news/timstanley/100261121/hitler-wasnt-a-socialist-stop-saying-he-was/
[121] http://www.academia.edu/3983109/Democratic_Confederalism_as_a_Kurdish_Spring_the_PKK_and_the_quest_for_radical_democracy p.185

we would simply stop walking if we stopped seeking it out. While we might accidentally stumble towards a better world (or an even worse world), then, the only way to truly ensure some sort of advance (imperfect as it may be) is to keep walking towards the horizon (with our minds grounded in reason and evidence, of course). In the same way, while I have not sought to glorify the Rojava Revolution in this book, I do believe it takes us one step closer to the horizon, offering us hope for a better Middle East and a better world. It has its imperfections like all other political processes, but it is without a doubt a beautiful example of humanity's search for dignity, justice, equality, and freedom.

Essentially, what the Rojava Revolution and other attempts to forge direct democracy reveal to us is that, if people truly have total control over their own destinies and that of their community, they only have themselves to blame if they do not achieve what they want to achieve. If they delegate their destinies to others, however, they can seek to avoid blame, and thus avoid taking responsibility for their own lives, their own happiness, and the wellbeing of their communities. Therefore, the more control people have over their own lives, their own natural resources, their own land, and their own communities, the more they will develop as the creative human beings they have the potential to be. They will then experience first-hand the power of cooperation and the power of autonomy, which will in turn allow them to experience true freedom and true justice. And neither imperialists, nor nationalists, nor religious fundamentalists could ever bring all of this to the People. They need to demand it; take it; and build it with their own hands. And that is why the inhabitants of Rojava have not tried to take over the whole of Syria, and why they are focussing primarily on their own communities, because that is where true revolution begins – with autonomous control of one's own community.

The Rojava Revolution clearly represents humanity's search for equality, cooperation, peace, and justice. And that is why those of us who seek a better world should show solidarity with the progressives behind this experience. They are us, and we are them. Their eyes are on the horizon, just like ours, and if we move towards that horizon together in harmony with them, we will advance much further and much more quickly.

In this story, which is far from approaching its end, we will all need to be protagonists. For, without our participation, the ending is unlikely to look as we want it to look. Therefore, we must become more and more active in our search to ensure that it is we, the People, who determine the outcome of this wonderfully complex chronicle that is human existence.

For democracy and freedom;
For peace and justice;
For love and solidarity;
The struggle must continue.

Glossary of Abbreviations

AKP   The neoliberal Islamist ruling party in Turkey (2002-present), led by Recep Tayyip Erdoğan until 2014

DTK   The union of legal Kurdish organisations in Turkey

HDK   The union of legal left-wing organisations in Turkey

HDP   A secular, feminist, and left-wing coalition party in Turkey

KCK   The union of illegal Kurdish organisations in the Middle East

KRG   The autonomous Kurdish Regional Government of Iraq, run by corrupt nationalists since 2004

PKK   The Kurdistan Workers' Party (formed in 1978), which is mainly active in Turkey and Iraq

PYD   The Democratic Union Party (the PKK's allies in Syria and the pioneers of the Rojava Revolution)

TEV-DEM The Movement for a Democratic Society: the left-wing, multi-ethnic coalition (including the PYD) at the heart of the bottom-up Rojava Revolution

YPG   Created after 2004 as armed wing of PYD, it is the official defence force of the Rojava Revolution, together with the YPJ

YPJ   Created in 2012 as the all-female equivalent of the YPG

Final Note: This book summary has not been published for profit, but with the intention of increasing the reader's knowledge and understanding of the topics discussed. While I have at no point sought to appropriate the work of other writers, the references (accessed between August 2014 and October 2015) are primarily for the benefit of the reader rather than for the benefit of copyright laws. At the same time, I am confident in claiming that the assertions and arguments made in this book are both verifiable and justifiable. For the complete evidence and reasoning behind my words, though, along with the comments of a significant number of progressive activists, journalists, and academics, I encourage you to read and analyse the full, in-depth investigation in my book.[122]

---

[122] https://ososabiouk.wordpress.com/2015/04/07/pdf-of-rojava-an-alternative-to-imperialism-nationalism-and-islamism-in-the-middle-east/

68220840R00072

Made in the USA
Lexington, KY
05 October 2017